To Chris
Best wishes
Robert C Baxley

THE LIFEGUARDS

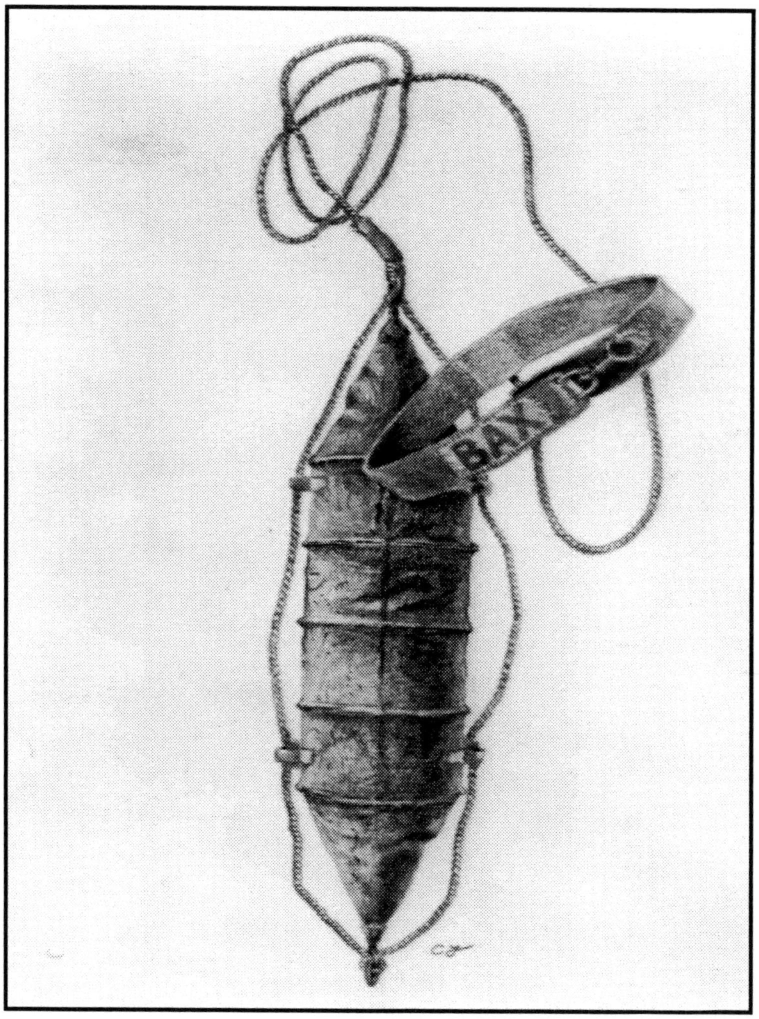

By

Robert C. Baxley

A publication of the Sunset Cliff Literary, Poetry and Philosophical Society

Printed in the United States of America
October 1998

ISBN 1-889553-11-5

Cover illustrations and those inside the book are by Charles Faust
Cover Graphics are by Kathleen Blavatt
Printed by WhitMar Electronic Press, El Cajon, CA.

LIST OF CONTENTS

If you don't know where you are going,
You will probably get there!
(Anonymous)

San Diego Lifeguard Relay Champions 1958

Dedication

As its name implies, Ocean Beach, California, is a small, self-contained beach town situated just north of the Point Loma lighthouse and about 15 miles from the Mexican border. In the early days, beach-goers were protected by a small, select group of watermen.

Although, as far as I know he never came to Ocean Beach probably the most famous lifeguard in recorded history was Duke Paoa Kahanamoku. The Duke first came to Southern California around 1912 and introduced the sport of board surfing to what was then just a sleepy beach community. His demonstrations of standing on water sparked the interest of local beach boys, who now were interested in learning how to "surf."

Not as well known as his surfing was a rescue the Duke made later, on June 14, 1925, at Corona del Mar, about 100 miles north of Ocean Beach. On a day when the beach was closed out by huge waves, Duke and some of his surfing friends were hanging out on the sand when they saw the sport fisher "Thelma" with a boatload of passengers, foundering in the surf line. As they watched, a giant set caught and capsized the boat, throwing its twenty-nine passengers overboard into the foam. Duke grabbed his board and paddled through the huge surf toward the disaster. Using his surfboard as a flotation device, he was able to save twelve of the passengers. The others all drowned, many having been knocked unconscious when the boat overturned and they were thrown into the water. This was the first dramatic statement (at least in Southern California) of the potential value of using surfboards in ocean rescues.

The early surfboards, called planks, were aptly named as they were wide, usually over twelve feet long and weighed over one-hundred pounds. Made of redwood, they had oak stringers in the center and along the sides and a small skeg at the back. The boards were varnished to keep the wood from soaking up too much ocean.

It was easy to get a "plank" into a wave, and because it was so big and heavy, the surfer could be standing and riding the swell even before it started to break. The plank rode well in a straight line, but was difficult to turn, requiring the surfer to drag a foot in the water to initiate a change in that direction.

These early surfers became accomplished rough water swimmers because, with leashes an invention for the future, they spent a lot of time swimming after their boards. They quickly learned the advantage of using the swift rip currents to get out to the break and, when knocked off their boards, of swimming with the breaking surf to quickly get to shore (and retrieve their boards). Most of the early Ocean Beach/Sunset Cliffs surfers went on to become excellent ocean lifeguards because of their developed swimming strength and first-hand knowledge of waves and rip currents, gained through their surfing adventures.

Spade Burns

This book is dedicated to my fellow lifeguards, to Duke Kahanamoku, who taught us how to be guards, and to those legendary pioneer Ocean Beach-Sunset Cliffs surfer/lifeguards who showed us the way. Although they had no formal lifeguard training, their knowledge of the local surf, tides and currents was unique, and they set the standard for those of us who followed.

Ocean Beach, 1941

Introduction

This is an account of my life on the beach in the 1950's, mostly at Ocean Beach in San Diego, California. Ocean Beach lies just north of the entrance to San Diego Harbor and south of the channel that leads from the ocean to Mission Bay. It was, and still is, a popular place for local beach-goers.

The strip of sand that locals refer to as Ocean Beach is along the ocean side of the Point Loma peninsula, generally bounded by Point Loma Avenue on the south and the Mission Bay channel on the north. Extending south from Ocean Beach are the Sunset Cliffs. As indicated by their name, the area is suitable mostly for surfers and divers, as the cliffs provide steep, muddy access to their rocky base. As there is almost no beach, it is an area to be avoided by the faint-of-heart.

The swimming area at Ocean Beach is about three quarters of a mile long, extending south from the Silver Spray Hotel at the foot of Niagara Street to the rock jetty that protects the Mission Bay Channel. Because of the cliffs and reefs to the south, more reefs that run parallel to the beach, and the Mission Bay jetty, Ocean Beach is considered one of the most dangerous swimming beaches in California. Statistics show that, each year, more "real" rescues are made here than at all other swimming beaches in California combined.

In the fifties, Ocean Beach was a crime-free, family-oriented community where residents took pride in their homes, businesses and their idyllic location on this small corner of the planet. The old lifeguard station, with its circular driveway, was located on the beach at the end of Santa Monica Avenue and just one block north of Newport Avenue, the community's "main drag."

On the beach about fifty feet south of the lifeguard station were three little buildings, aligned with a surveyor's precision between the ocean and Santa Monica Avenue, so that only the first one had an unobstructed view of the sea. The building nearest the street was Mrs. Miller's hamburger stand. In the middle was a small cottage, and the third structure, right on the sand, was the "Beach Hut."

To the north of the lifeguard station was the old "merry-go-round" building, which no longer deserved its name, as the carousel was long gone. By then it housed May's hamburger stand and Noel's used furniture.

During the forties, and maybe even the thirties, the lifeguard station served as both a police substation and lifeguard tower. By the fifties, though, the police had moved on, and the entire building had been taken over by the lifeguards, although the police still kept a desk and typewriter for preparing reports. The Ocean Beach lifeguard station also housed the cliff rescue truck, a surf dory and, most importantly, a kitchen. During evenings when the moon and tide were out, the station became a local entertainment center.

This book deals with some of the more remarkable events that occurred during this time and in this space. I have tried to recount these events as accurately as possible, asking the reader's indulgence for some exaggeration that may have occurred due to my memory and to the passage of time. The names of persons who might be embarrassed by some of the accounts have been changed to protect me from libel suits. The names of others, who might be proud of their participation, or who have nothing to gain by protecting their reputations, are real.

Marsh Malcolm, James Robb, Bob Figer

Nothing but the wind,
can pass the sun without
leaving a shadow.

(Charlie Chan)

My brother Neil, mother, and me (Bax), 1938

Chapter 1

Before I Was a Lifeguard

By contemporary standards of the ideal, my childhood left much to be desired. Looking back, though, it doesn't seem so bad.

I was five in 1934 when my father abandoned us and left my mother to raise my older brother and me alone. The task eventually became too much for her, and she had such a severe breakdown that she was committed to a state mental hospital. I was sent to a foster home to live with "Ma" Smith and her husband in Ranchita, a ranching community near the Borrego Desert in southeastern San Diego County.

It was a new life for me, a kid from the beach on a working ranch in an arid landscape. There were usually one or two other foster children, and I had to earn my keep as they did. When I wasn't in school, I milked cows, fed cattle, cut brush, and shoveled out barns and stalls. I did as I was told, as I was afraid of Mrs. Smith. I don't remember her ever doing anything bad, but I was afraid of her anyway.

I left that life as soon as I could. In August 1945, just after my seventeenth birthday, I enlisted in the Army Air Force and was stationed in San Antonio, Texas. Discharged in 1949, I returned to San Diego and resumed my real life — near the ocean.

But there is more to the story. Before my mother got sick, we lived on the bay side of Mission Beach in a converted garage. Mission Beach was a sand peninsula three miles long and two-hundred yards wide that separated the Pacific Ocean from Mission Bay. On the ocean side, a solid sea wall kept the surf from washing over the peninsula. This sea wall, built by the WPA during the Great Depression, has stood the test of both ocean.

At the south end of the peninsula, where water from the ocean enters the bay, a bridge crossed the channel, connecting the rest of the world and Mission Beach to Ocean Beach. In addition to cars and trucks, the trolley crossed the bridge on its way between downtown San Diego and La Jolla. A pedestrian walkway was used by fishermen and locals who threw spears at unfortunate fish that swam under the bridge in clear view, to become someone's next meal.

In the thirties, Mission Bay was an unspoiled, natural fish and game preserve. The main channel ran from south to north, from the entrance to the bay to about where the Hotel Catamaran is today. Throughout the shallow bay were acres of high weeds and tributaries of water. Ducks and geese were plentiful. Fish, scallops, clams and other sea life were abundant. All were hunted and harvested for food by local residents.

It was in this setting, after my father had abandoned us, that Charlie Wright taught me to swim. Charlie was a healthy, solid, kind man in his late forties. To me, he looked real rugged. At one time he had been a stunt man in the movies, and to all the local kids he was a hero. And for a fatherless five-year-old, he was just what the doctor ordered.

To keep the neighborhood children from drowning, Charlie decided to teach us all how to swim. His house was on the bay, and it had a pier with a big float attached. Charlie's method was to take one of us down to the float and tie a wide canvas belt around our waist. The belt was attached to a rope. At the other end of the rope was an enormous (or so it seemed) bamboo pole. Charlie would drop the swimmer-of-the-day into the bay and swing him in a large arc on the surface, shouting instructions. After several sessions, Charlie secretly released the tension on the rope. We would be swimming on our own, without knowing it. When he thought we were ready, Charlie would point out that the support no longer came from the bamboo pole. And we were swimming! The resulting dog paddle and our lack of endurance both required some fine-tuning, but we were now "waterproof" and in no imminent danger of drowning. One by one, Charlie got each of us comfortable in the water, and then we were on our own.

Since I didn't have a bike, baseball equipment, or much of anything else, and I could now "swim," my principal diversion was to float along with the outgoing and incoming tides. The trick on the outgoing tide was to hit the beach before I was swept under the bridge and hooked or speared by someone fishing from the pedestrian walkway, or before I was swept to sea on an outgoing swell.

Then I learned to dive. Some older boys in the neighborhood had made a diving helmet out of an old water heater. They attached a length of garden hose to the heater and used a tire pump to force air into it. The "helmet" then sat on our shoulders. When we went under, we hoped our tender could pump enough air into the helmet to keep the water level below the glass port and give us enough air to breathe. I never went very deep and always had to abandon the helmet to keep from drowning.

From this, I progressed to a pair of makeshift goggles that someone had thrown into one of those big trash barrels on the beach. The goggles sort of worked, so I wore them when I floated with the tides. Now, during my drifting, I could actually see what was in the water. Soon I was gathering clams and scallops, and trying to spear fish. In those days, very few people ate that stuff; had there been a market for it, I could have supported my mother and brother quite well. It wasn't long until, swimming with my new goggles, I ventured from the bay side to the ocean side of the peninsula where I now learned to gather Pismo clams and spear corvina.

The converted garage where we lived was near the Old Mission Beach lifeguard tower, which then was in the middle of the business district. The lifeguard assigned to this tower was called "Goggy", a childhood mispronunciation of "Gregory," his real name. Goggy was tan and blond and the idol of the college crowd that claimed that section of beach. He spent most of his on-duty time posing for admirers.

One day, when I was about eight, I got caught in a rip current right in front of the lifeguard tower. I struggled for what seemed like hours as I tried to swim toward shore, only to be dragged out by the current, gasping for air and flailing against the force of the ocean. I thought I was going to drown, but finally thrashed my way back to the beach. I remember lying on the sand, exhausted, when Goggy finally came up and nudged me with his toe. I guess he wanted to see if I was still alive. He asked me what had happened, and when I told my story, he said I was stupid. Then he explained how to swim parallel to the shore to get out of a rip if I was caught in one again.

His advice has served me well, and I never had any more trouble with rip currents. I remember thinking at the time that Goggy must have been too busy with his admirers to see a child out in the ocean, struggling against the surf.

Although I had no way of knowing it then, these early experiences were the stepping stones to my becoming a lifeguard. This of course happened after I left the Air Force and returned to San Diego.

Don't tell people your troubles.
Half don't care, and the other half
are glad you're getting
what's coming to you.
(Elbert Hubbard)

Ocean Beach Lifeguard Station, 1942

Chapter 2

May and Mrs. Miller

On either side of the lifeguard station, at the entrance that faces Abbot Street, two hamburger stands competed for business from the beach-going public. There was no "inside" to these places, just a food preparation area surrounded by a serving counter, across which food and drinks were passed to barefoot patrons.

May's stand was located north of the lifeguard station in a corner of the old merry-go-round building. Across the lifeguard station driveway to the south, Mrs. Miller had her stand in one of the three little cottages that ran between Santa Monica Avenue and the ocean.

May was a thin, older woman, a heavy smoker and drinker who looked like something you might find in a bait store. She had been there for many years and without any competition, until Mrs. Miller arrived.

Mrs. Miller was a cute, chubby little Jewish grandmother who spoke with an accent and had a sister who could have been her twin. It became clear during her first month of operation that Mrs. Miller had both the resources and the desire to put May out of business. She started a price war.

Hamburgers went from thirty five cents to thirty cents. In a countermove, May reduced her hamburger prices to twenty-five cents. These moves and countermoves continued until late August. By then, you could buy a hamburger from Mrs. Miller for ten cents.

For May, the ten-cent hamburger was the final straw. She had taken all she could! Fortunately, I was in the back of the station the day when, armed with a butcher knife, May headed for Mrs. Miller's stand. At the same time, Mrs. Miller also was advancing, wielding a cast iron skillet. I watched as the two women, with weapons raised, closed the distance between them, clearly ready to engage in physical violence. My responsibility as caretaker of the beach was clear, so at considerable risk to my own safety, I intervened and prevented what surely would have been a tragedy.

May held on through the summer, and at the end of the season closed her stand for the last time.

For a few memorable weeks, those of us in Ocean Beach had enjoyed the best prices on hamburgers in the United States.

Going somewhere
but not really caring where.

(Vautar)

Chapter 3

Malcolm the Mooch

Annie lived next to the lifeguard station with her very beautiful and very large dog "Malcolm". The locals referred to him as a poi, Hawaiian slang for a dog of unknown lineage. Although Malcolm looked like a wonderful dog, in reality he was evil and sneaky. Eventually Annie had to move away from the beach. For some reason, she couldn't take Malcolm with her, so she tried to find him a suitable home. She went everywhere and asked everyone, but without success. It was apparent that nobody wanted Malcolm. Looking back, I am sure all the people Annie tried to pass him off on knew a great deal more than I did.

Finally, time ran out for Annie and Malcolm, so she begged me to keep the dog, just until a home could be found. For some reason, I agreed. Big mistake!

As soon as Annie had moved away, I began to discover the truth about Malcolm. The first time I let him out to "get some exercise" (and every time thereafter), he was off down the beach and out of sight, to be captured by the folks at Animal Control. After awhile, I had so many calls from the pound that the conversation was always the same:

"Ocean Beach Lifeguard Station, Baxley speaking."

"Hey, Bax, this is Joe at the pound. We've got Malcolm again!"

"OK, I'll be over to get him."

Another thing about Malcolm was his unique beach

technique. Crawling on his belly, as though if he were near the ground nobody would see him, the dog would sneak across the sand to someone's blanket or towel when the intended victim was out swimming. Malcolm would eat whatever food was there, then piss on the blanket and run away. I tell you, that dog was evil!

During the few weeks I had Malcolm, my bill at Mrs. Miller's skyrocketed because I felt obliged to buy hamburgers and cokes for all of his victims.

One day, as summer was ending, my prayers were answered. A nice, unsuspecting family visiting California from the Midwest happened to stop by the lifeguard station where Malcolm was lying in the shade, tied to our jeep. As soon as the children saw him, they ran over to pet him and make a big fuss over the huge dog. It is important to note here that Malcolm, when he wanted to, could be a real charmer, and he really turned it on for this family! When the carousing canine was at his peak of charm and the children were falling in love with him, I dropped my bomb: "Would you like to have him?" There was a uniform cry of, "Yes!" from mother and children.

About this time the father arrived, and the mother and children immediately began begging to take Malcolm. The father relented under the onslaught, and I watched as they drove away, with Malcolm and the family happily together in the car.

I never again saw the family or the dog. But I'm sure that at the first rest stop, Malcolm ran off and the family spent hours trying to catch him, if they ever did.

We live, as we dream-alone.
(Joseph Conrad)

Chapter 4

Little Mike

He appeared one spring day, a skinny little eight-year-old with thick glasses. He hung out at the beach for about a year, and during the entire time, I never saw him with anyone. He was always alone. He would arrive about ten in the morning, carrying his lunch, and he would stay until about four in the afternoon. He never talked to other kids. Most of the time he would just swing on an old tire that hung from a rope on the chinning bar on the beach north of the lifeguard tower. I tried talking to him, but the most I ever got was his first name, "Mike."

Each day, Mike carried his lunch in a brown paper bag, which he placed carefully on the ground beside him while he was swinging in the tire. One day, Malcolm, the evil Airedale, got hold of his lunch and ran off with it. As I watched from my station on the beach, "Little Mike" just stood there, kicking at the sand and rubbing his fists into his eyes so nobody could see he was crying. He was so upset that I took him by the hand to Mrs. Miller's and treated him to a hamburger and coke. That seemed to cheer him and almost bond us, but still there was no conversation from Little Mike.

Another day I was watching Mike swing in the tire and saw him get tangled in the loose end of the rope until he was hanging about a foot off the ground. He just couldn't get unraveled, no matter how hard he tried. I watched him thrash around for what seemed like a very long time, expecting him to yell for help. But he didn't. Finally, when I could no longer bear to watch him struggle, I walked over and cut the rope. Mike thumped down onto the sand. Once on the ground, he extricated himself from the rope and ran off without a word.

The final incident with Little Mike happened when he was out swimming. He got himself caught in a hole so deep that he couldn't get free of the current to swim to shore. I watched him struggle, certain that the situation would prompt him to call out for assistance. Not my Little Mike. Finally, I walked out into the water, grabbed his hand, and brought him to shore. He almost, but not quite, thanked me.

And that was the last time I saw him. Over the years I have often thought of Little Mike and wondered what happened to him.

I would like to meet him again, just to see how he's doing.

Always do right!
This gratifies some people
and astonishes the rest.
(Mark Twain)

Charles W. Hardy

Chapter 5

Charles W. Hardy: Our Captain

He was born in 1909, went to work as a lifeguard in 1930 when the lifeguards were part of the Police Department, and became Captain in 1940. He died young, in February 1968, while still the Lifeguard Captain.

In 1946 the lifeguards were transferred to the Park and Recreation Department. I went to work for the San Diego City Lifeguards in 1952, with Charles W. Hardy as my Captain. Tall, muscular, ruggedly handsome and sun-bleached, he had spent his whole life on the beach. The Captain also was a heavy drinker, beginning his consumption about ten each morning. In the entire time I worked for the lifeguards, I can't recall seeing him out of his black shirt and long pants, as he no longer had active "guard duty." During all our years of service together, I know of only one occasion when the booze may have interfered with his professional competence. He was distant and aloof with most guards, but I soon found that good food was the way to his heart.

Rumors about Captain Hardy's success with women in his early days were legend, although he was too much of a gentleman to talk about it. Only once, after we had become friends, did he comment to me in private, "Same way too, Bub, if I told you the names of all the society women I've slept with in this town, it would blow the lid right off the social register." At the time, I didn't think he was bragging. I still don't.

The Ocean Beach lifeguard station occupied the building that had once served as both police substation and lifeguard tower. When the police gave up the substation, the lifeguards took over. The old jail cell was converted into a shower. The office was unchanged, although we added a couch. There were two garages, a first aid room and a kitchen. The back of the station, facing the street, housed the cliff rig, and the front, facing the beach, housed the dory. By the time of this story, Captain Hardy had shifted his main interest from women to food. And how he did love to eat! Especially abalone sandwiches on sourdough bread.

Old Mission Beach Lifeguard Station, 1952

Fortunately, abalone were abundant in the area, and my daily dives produced a ready supply, which I cooked up in our kitchen. After learning of Captain Hardy's new lust, I soon became a trusted and favorite employee, which meant he never tried to catch me not doing my duty, and he never arrived at Ocean Beach unannounced, as he did at some other stations.

He would call me about ten each morning, and the conversation went something like this:

"Ocean Beach Lifeguard Station, Baxley speaking."

"Jesus Christ, same way too, Bub, what's up for lunch today, Bub?"

"Well, Captain, I went diving this morning and got some fresh abalone."

"Same way too, Bub. I'll bring the bread."

He would arrive promptly on schedule, and the feast would begin. Usually he had three sandwiches, but on one occasion (I think he was depressed), I remember him eating seven.

Only once was our daily luncheon ritual in jeopardy, based on the success or failure of our newest brainchild, the season-ending lifeguard relays.

It all began one uneventful day while sitting in the tower with Don Mellon, a brother lifeguard. We were watching it rain. Having nothing better to do, we decided it would be great if we had a water competition at the end of each summer to cap off the season. Our idea was to pit the South Division lifeguards (Ocean Beach, Mission Beach and Pacific Beach) against the North Division guards (La Jolla, which had a similar number of stations). We presented our plan to Captain Hardy and the lifeguard lieutenants, who all bought into the idea.

Then we got busy planning. We scheduled the event for the last Friday in August. It would begin at six in the evening at lifeguard headquarters in the Mission Beach amusement center. The competition would consist of a medley relay of three events, with each lifeguard limited to participating in one event. In the end, there were two teams, each with twelve lifeguards.

For the first event, a relay team of four lifeguards, each

towing a rescue buoy, would swim around a marker one-hundred-fifty yards offshore. In those days, the rescue buoy was a two-foot metal cylinder with a four-foot rope attached at one end and a belt that went around the lifeguard's waist at the other. For the second event, another four-lifeguard relay team would paddle their rescue surfboards out around the same marker buoy. For the final event, two teams would row a dory out around the buoy. Of these events, the most difficult and hazardous was the dory competition.

Winning San Diego Lifeguard Relays Team, 1958

As race day neared, I called the Captain and suggested we have a celebrity judge for our contest. He liked the idea and assigned me to find someone appropriate. First I called the mayor, but he was otherwise engaged. Next I called the city manager, Hump Campbell (the big boss). Happily, he agreed to officiate our event. When the day arrived, Captain Hardy asked me if I had found a judge.

When I told him who it was, he and Don Vinn (the head of aquatics) went into shock. Captain Hardy said to me, "You've gone too far this time, Baxley." No "Bub," a sure sign he was pissed!

Thinking about it for the first time, I could guess why. Everyone, including the Captain, knew that Don Vinn was building a boat in the lifeguard station, on city time, with the help of the lifeguard carpenter and the city's tools. And we also knew of Captain Hardy's drinking habits. So my little plan was jeopardizing our low profile. The last thing Hardy and Vinn needed was someone from the city to disrupt their peaceful existence.

As a result, the mood was very tight that evening but, fortunately for me, the relays were a success, and Hump loved them. I don't know if he discovered any of our unusual operating procedures, but nothing was ever said. I became a hero instead of a goat, and Captain Hardy did not banish me to the dreaded Bonito Basin which was the childrens area on the bay side behind lifeguard headquarters. That was where lifeguards who had made unpardonable mistakes were sent, where there were no cute teenage girls, only mothers with screaming children.

My candle burns at both ends,
it will not last the night;
but oh my foes and oh my friends
it gives a lovely light.
(Edna St. Vincent Millay)

Maynard and Marion Heatherly at WindinSea

Chapter 6

Maynard

He was a lifeguard at Ocean Beach in the late forties and early fifties. All the kids loved him. Even the sand crabs liked Maynard. He later worked at Lifeguard Headquarters at the Mission Beach Amusement Center in South Mission Beach.

Maynard Heatherly was a six-foot-two-inch blond god who made Johnny Weismuller look plain, and he was married to the reigning beauty queen of San Diego. He was a swimmer and fearless in the water. But there was something else about Maynard . . . it seemed he wasn't hitting on all cylinders.

One day in the early fifties, before the Mission Bay Channel was dredged, a boat overturned at the ocean entrance to the channel, killing several of its passengers. In response to public outcry, the City of San Diego closed the channel to incoming and outgoing boat traffic. A lifeguard station was built on the edge of the jetty at the north end of Mission Boulevard to keep boats away from the channel entrance, and the lifeguards kept a power boat, the "Alert," at a nearby dock. The station was open twenty-four hours a day, seven days a week and operated three shifts: eight in the morning until four in the afternoon, four to midnight, and midnight to eight. Roger Grady was permanently assigned to the day shift and was the boat operator.

One very foggy night in May, Maynard was working the swing shift. About nine in the evening, Roger came back to the tower for something he had forgotten during the day and was surprised to find the building empty. Roger searched for Maynard but couldn't find him anywhere and then noticed that one of the rescue buoys was missing. The rule in those days was, if an emergency called the lifeguard away from the station, the guard was to call and notify another guard of the situation. That other guard usually was Roger, because he was permanently assigned the day shift. But Roger had not been notified, so he decided to investigate. He found the keys to the Alert and took the boat out into the channel.

The tide was going out as Roger slowly headed toward the ocean, yelling Maynard's name. Once outside the safety of the channel, Roger started to turn around when, in the darkness, he heard Maynard yelling for help. He eased the Alert toward the sound and found Maynard and a woman clinging to the rescue buoy. Roger picked them up, and they returned to the warmth of the lifeguard station.

Maynard related to Roger that he had been on the tower when he heard cries for help. Without thinking or stopping to call, he grabbed a rescue buoy, dove off the jetty into the channel and was being swept to sea on the outgoing tide when, by chance, he drifted by the woman. She and her boyfriend had been having frantic sex on the rocks when they fell into the water and were caught in the outgoing tide.

By the time Maynard reached the woman, her boyfriend was nowhere to be found. He knew that, once outside the channel, they would have to either swim north and then in through the surf north of the channel or wait for the tide to change and drift back in the channel. This was about the time Roger found them.

Several days later, the boyfriend's body was found. It was determined he had drowned.

Later, Maynard submitted a dramatized account of the event to "Heroic Comics," who published his version of the rescue.

Another time, while working at lifeguard headquarters, Maynard suddenly came running from somewhere in the back of the station, probably the locker room, with a rescue buoy clanging along behind him on its rope.

As the story goes, Maynard sprinted out of the building, with the can noisily bouncing along like a small dog, and headed north along the walk next to the sea wall. No one on the beach understood the urgency and just watched as he ran along, jumped over the sea wall, ran across the sand and dove into the water. They watched Maynard swim out to a small child who was headed to sea in a rip current, a child nobody else had even seen. How Maynard knew the child was out there was a mystery. But he seemed to have a sixth sense about those things.

After he retired from lifeguarding, Maynard disappeared to Australia for several years. When he returned, it was without his beautiful wife, who had left him for someone else. Maynard had let his blond hair grow to his substantial shoulders and wore an Australian bush hat. With a silent partner, he opened a beer bar on the alley behind the entrance to Crystal Pier in Pacific Beach, where he now spoke pidgin English and served twenty-five-cent breakfasts on paper plates in the alley behind the bar.

One time he got into a rhubarb with the police, who were going to arrest him, so he escaped by running out to the end of

Crystal Pier and diving off, hitting his head. He almost drowned that day. Shortly after the incident, Maynard did die, from a brain tumor. Some speculate the tumor was the explanation for Maynard's always somewhat bizarre behavior. I don't subscribe to that. I just think he was different. Anyway, things at the beach were never the same after Maynard was gone.

Lamar Boren, 1950

Chapter 7

Lamar "Pops" Boren

I don't remember how I first met him, but even before I did, I knew Lamar Boren was a famous underwater cinematographer and a member of the "Bottom Scratchers," the first organized skin diving club in the United States. Along with Lamar, two other early members of the Bottom Scratchers were San Diegans Jack Padonovich (1933) and Wally Potts (1939). Jack was the janitor at Point Loma High School. On the side, he designed and manufactured spear guns. Wally was his diving partner and an engineer at Solar. In their time, they were two of the best free divers in the world. They both still live in Ocean Beach, and Jack still makes spears that are used by many of the best open water spear fishermen.

Lamar Boren, Shelter Island, 1953

Lamar, or "Pops," as I called him, was a giant in both stature and heart. He and his own son were estranged, so he sort of adopted me.

One summer when I was lifeguarding at

Ocean Beach, I came down with mononucleosis and was bed-ridden in my little shack by the lifeguard station. When Lamar found out I was so sick, he took me to his home in North Park where he and his wife nursed me until I recovered. Afterward, he was always "Pops" to me.

His strength in the water was legendary. He easily managed the big, cumbersome underwater cameras of the day. While most men staggered under their weight and bulk, Pops handled them without seeming to notice.

Pops was the photographer who filmed most of the important underwater sequences for television and movies at that time. His credits included "Sea Hunt" with Lloyd Bridges, "Underwater" with Jane Russell and Richard Egan, and "The Old Man and the Sea," with Spencer Tracy.

I made many dives with Pops and never saw him wear a wetsuit, regardless of the task or temperature of the water. Once we blew up the reef at Dana Point so the city could install a new sewer outfall line. Another time we tested a new regulator. We went down to two hundred feet, and we each used an entire tank of air. But Pops never wore a wetsuit.

I once worked as a grip for Pops to help him handle the camera while shooting an underwater sequence for a movie. Out on the water in the support boat, it was my job to get into the water first and hold the camera while Pops got into the water, which was about three hundred feet deep under the boat.

The camera and housing weighed over one hundred pounds, with a tank at the top that could be inflated with compressed air.

In the water, the camera operator turned on the air valve to fill the housing to the point of neutral buoyancy so the camera would be manageable. The trick was to turn the valve quickly, as the weight of the camera would send it and the operator on a rapid descent toward the ocean floor.

When Pops leaned out of the boat and handed me the camera, my hand slipped off the valve. I struggled to maintain control, at the same time searching for the valve with my hand. The camera and I plummeted down about two hundred feet before I could turn the valve and get enough air into the chamber to equalize the camera's buoyancy. At the time, I wasn't really concerned for my own safety. I knew if I dropped the camera, I might as well just keep going down, because I was more afraid of what would happen if I came up without it. But I finally got the valve turned on, and with the camera now buoyant, we (the camera and I) drifted up to the surface for a successful day's shoot.

Lamar died in 1986 after a brilliant career as a cinematographer in Television and Movies.

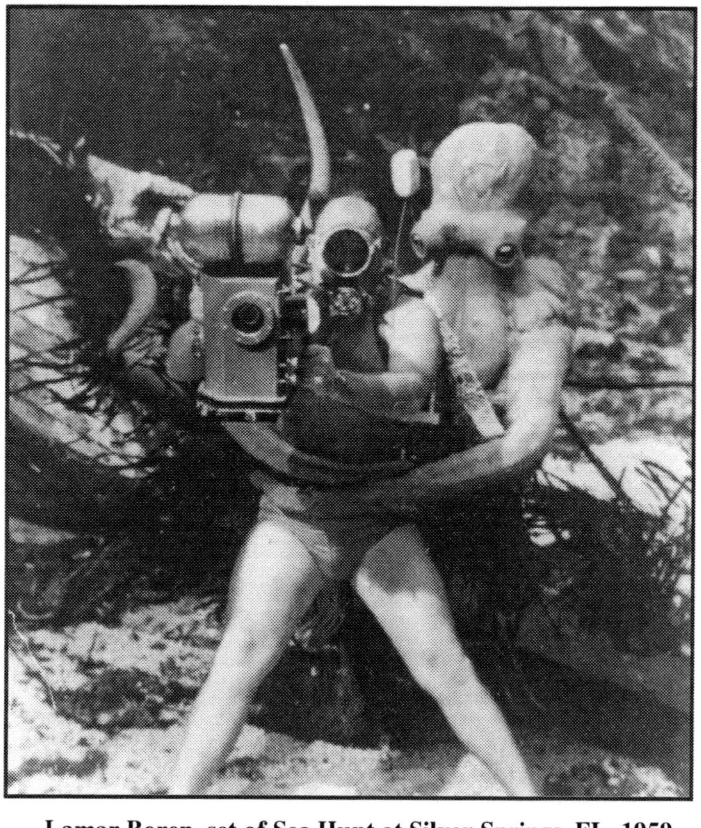

Lamar Boren, set of Sea Hunt at Silver Springs, FL, 1959

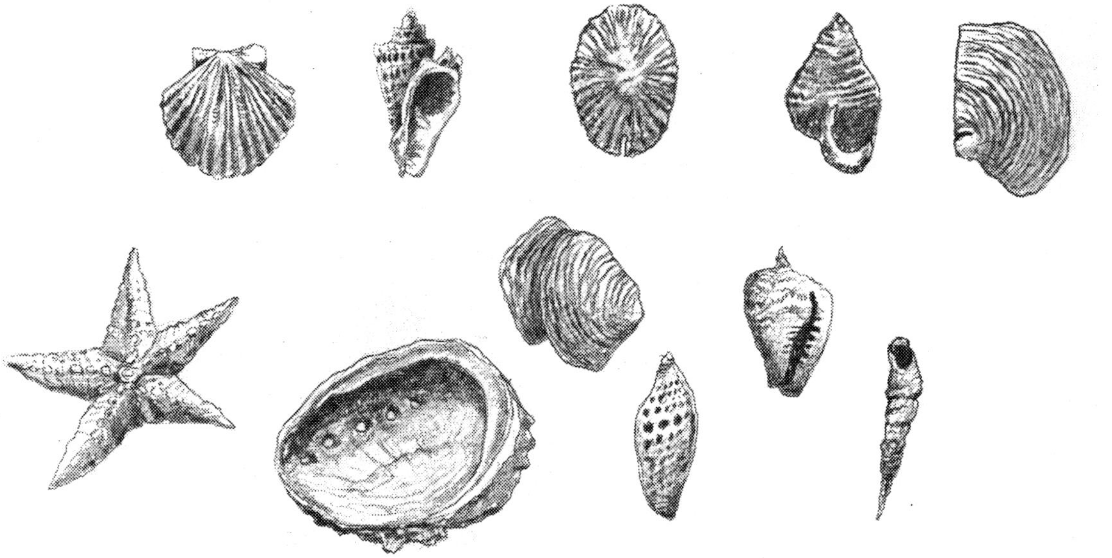

Chapter 8

Leonard Cooper

Leonard Cooper was a lifeguard. He was tall and lanky and wore a braided ponytail (a real annoyance to Captain Hardy). He drove a motorcycle, and his hands were always greasy. He wore thick glasses, and I always wondered how he had passed the lifeguard test, which included the requirement for all applicants to swim five hundred meters in a straight line.

Leonard worked at Ocean Beach for one summer. He never said much, and he never went drinking with us after work. But I liked Leonard.

Most guards hated tower duty. It was hot up there, and when you were on duty, you had to stay inside and just watch the water. It was better to be on beach duty, where it was cooler, and where you could check out the girls and get wet once in a while. But, as it turned out, the tower was the best place for Leonard Cooper.

One day when I was on tower duty, I saw a woman in trouble in the rip off the Silver Spray Hotel, about one-and-a-half blocks north of the tower. I called down to Leonard, who was the guard on the beach, to make the rescue. He responded immediately, tossing his glasses aside and running toward the water. From the tower, I watched him swim out toward the woman. Then I watched him swim past the victim to a spot where he thought she was and swim around, looking for her and yelling.

So much for my own tower duty. I yelled for Doug, the other

guard on the beach, to hook up the dory, and we started down the beach with it. We launched the boat and rowed to where the woman was still struggling in the rip. We hauled her into the boat, rowed back to the beach, and deposited her safely on the sand.

Then we checked the water. Leonard the lifeguard was still out there, still swimming and still looking for his rescue. I considered just letting him continue to search. Instead, we rowed out to tell him what had happened.

By the time we got to Leonard, he was tired and worried. We told him we had found the woman, so he could swim back to the beach. And we now knew that, without his glasses, Leonard was unable to see much of anything.

After that incident, Leonard wisely spent most of his time in the tower, wearing his glasses and watching the water for us. He did not return the following summer.

***Front seldom tells the truth.
To know the occupants of a house
always look in the back yard.***
(Charlie Chan)

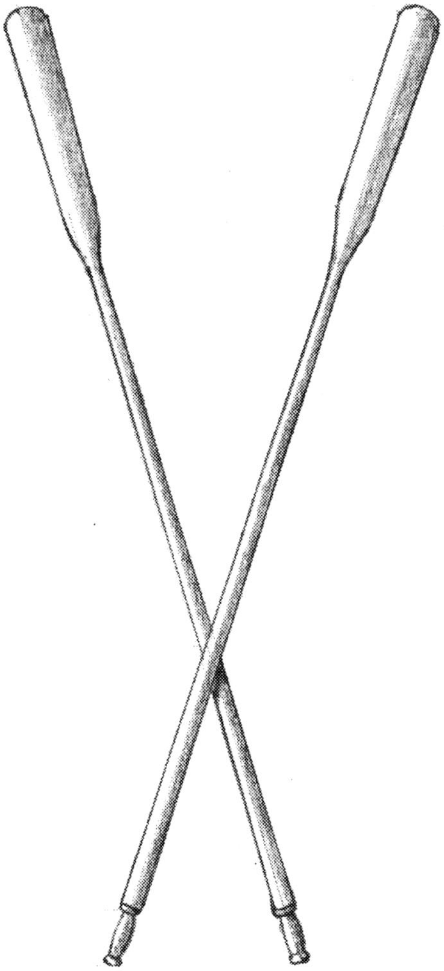

Chapter 9

Big Frank and the Bamboo by the Sea

A flagpole rises from the corner of Newport Avenue and Abbot Street. The lifeguard station is a block to the north and diagonally from a big lot on the northeast corner of Newport and Abbot, the site of a long, low, wooden building that housed a beer bar called "The Bamboo by the Sea." The length of the building was toward the ocean, with large, hinged windows on the beach side that swung open from the bottom. These were opened on hot days to take advantage of the cool onshore breezes.

Because the bar was owned by a Hawaiian named Dewey, it was frequented by the "south sea island" crowd. Many of the musicians from a local restaurant, the Bali Ha'i — Mona, Dewey, Henry, Tea, Kimo and Clarence — hung out at the Bamboo on summer weekends. In addition, Samoans, other south sea islanders and sailors from San Diego's huge contingent of Navy personnel comprised much of the clientele.

On most days and nights, music and laughter floated from the Bamboo. But on Saturdays, usually about sundown, there was the inevitable liquor-induced argument. It usually began with name-calling and then escalated into a full-scale brawl. The number and enthusiasm of participants would swell to fill the bar, then spill out through the windows, continuing the evening's fracas outside in the relative darkness. Inside, furniture and windows were normal casualties of the melee. Eventually, both the riot squad and shore patrol would arrive to haul the revelers to their appropriate destinations.

Always prepared, Dewey kept a ready supply of plywood that he nailed over the broken windows after such events. Then, for all the good it did, he locked up the place for the evening and went home. By the following Wednesday, Dewey would have replaced the glass and furniture and again be open for business.

When they were not drinking, the "islanders" who took advantage of Dewey's hospitality were kind, generous, fun-loving people who only wanted to enjoy the beach with their families. But their low tolerance for alcohol became readily apparent when Dewey's "kava" flowed too freely.

One of our local island characters was a huge Samoan we called "Big Frank," who stood nearly seven feet tall and weighed in at about three-hundred-fifty pounds. Most of Frank's front teeth were missing, and his nose went this way and that, obviously broken several times but never fixed. Although terrifying to look at, Frank was kind and peaceful when he was sober.

Each year at the onset of summer, the City of Ocean Beach would move temporary small, wooden lifeguard towers across the beach to be close to the water. At Ocean Beach, one of these portable structures would be placed directly in front of the permanent tower, which was on top of the old police substation. A second temporary tower would be placed in the center of the beach to the north. These towers were about eighteen feet high. The bottom was larger than the top and used for storage. The top of the portable towers had windows all around and just enough space for two lifeguards. A ladder on the outside provided access.

During the day, lifeguards would take shifts in these towers.

About four o'clock one hot Sunday afternoon, Greg Widders and I were serving our sentence in the tower in front of the main lifeguard station when the voice of a young woman below called up to us. I climbed down the ladder to the sand to find a very cute and highly agitated teenage girl. She said she and her friends were up the beach toward the Silver Spray Hotel and were being harassed by a drunk. I looked in the direction she pointed and saw Big Frank. "Shit," I thought, as my stomach sank to about the same level as my toes. I knew I had to do something about the three-hundred-plus-pound menace — after all, I was their lifeguard — but I wasn't sure what, without putting myself in considerable danger.

The girl and I started up the beach, in the direction of Big Frank. By the time we arrived, I still hadn't devised a plan, but instinctively I stood right up to Frank, nose-to-nose (or as much as my five-foot, ten-inch height would allow) and shook my finger at him, shouting, "If you don't leave these girls alone and behave yourself on my beach, I'm going to kick your Samoan ass from here to Samoa!" Then I turned on my heel and walked back to the tower. I climbed the ladder and, standing next to Greg, looked back to see what Frank was doing. He seemed to be planted in the same place I had encountered him, but with a puzzled look on his face.

At that instant, something inside Frank must have clicked, because he straightened up to his full height and, in a rage, started for the tower. I didn't have time to tell Greg what had happened, just that he should call the police. Then I jumped out the back of the tower, ran around the side away from Frank, sprinted across the beach into the water and swam out past the surf line. Once I was safe, I looked back to shore. The tower seemed to be swaying. Then I realized that Big Frank was shaking it while Greg, terrified, held on inside.

Fortunately, the police arrived before any damage was done to either Greg or the tower. They managed to subdue Big Frank and haul him off in handcuffs.

Understandably, Greg didn't speak to me for the rest of the summer. But Big Frank didn't cause any more trouble, either.

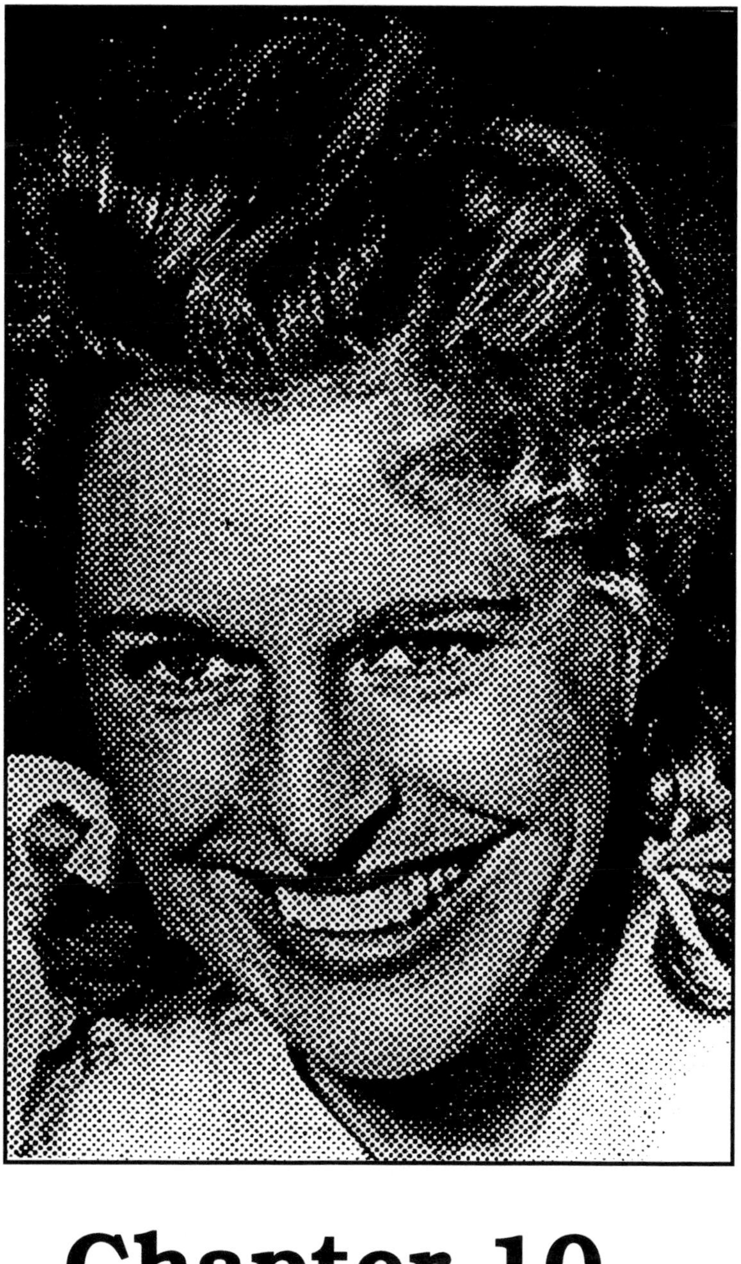

Chapter 10

Gena Grigg

Gena Grigg was the mother of Robin and Ricky Grigg, two of the most exceptional water persons I have ever known. Gena was a beautiful, dainty and, most of the time, refined woman in her mid-forties when I met the Grigg family. Mr. Grigg had been a screen writer. He died when Robin and Ricky were young. The Griggs lived at the beach in Santa Monica. Their house was on the north side of the sidewalk next to Little John's hamburger stand, between the patch of sand known everywhere as "Muscle Beach" and the Chase Hotel.

Ricky and Robin Grigg

Robin Grigg was the first great woman board surfer in California, and many believe the movie and television character, "Gidget," was patterned after her. She was tall, thin, beautiful and a great athlete. Her younger brother, Ricky, is one of the world's great watermen. Of all the water persons I have met or read about, Ricky is the finest. Like Robin, he was one of the world's great board surfers, a swimmer and lifeguard, an exceptional paddler and a deep sea diver. He became a renowned marine biologist.

But this is not about Robin or Ricky, it's about their mother, Gena.

One of my favorite stories about Gena was her confrontation with Little John, a huge man and retired professional wrestler. There were troubled relations between these two neighbors. Whenever Gena watered her front lawn, the excess drained across the walkway and formed a pool in front of Little John's hamburger stand, right where his customers would stand to place and receive their orders. This had been a sore spot for months between the giant ex-wrestler and the petite Gena Grigg. The two had exchanged words on many occasions.

One hot August Sunday, Gena was watering her grass, with the excess forming its characteristic puddle in front of the hamburger stand. Little John lost control and came out, swearing at Gena who, by now, had had enough of his verbal abuse. She turned the hose on the huge man, soaking him. During the commotion, a large crowd gathered to (hopefully) watch the beauty slay the beast, which she did.

But the incident and humiliation were more than Little John could endure, so he hired a lawyer and, in Santa Monica Superior Court, sued Gena for battery. Little John lost the case. Ironically, though, his business improved as a result of the publicity.

On another occasion, Robin, Ricky, Tad Devine, Willie Meyers and I spent several days diving in Baja. We acquired quite a stash of lobster and abalone, so we headed for the Grigg's house in Santa Monica for a feast. We arrived in the late afternoon and decided to have our party that evening. We encouraged Gena to invite her friends to help us consume the bounty.

Ricky and Tad, who never encountered anything he didn't know, decided to prepare a special South Sea Island punch for the event and immediately engaged in a huge argument about how to make it. Willie and I watched in amazement as the seriousness of the discussion escalated. After much turmoil, the ingredients for the huge bowl of punch were finally assembled and served to the guests. It was quickly consumed, followed by another loud and animated discussion and second bowl of punch. After this batch was made, dinner was served. Midway through dinner, the punch was again gone, and yet another bowl was needed.

By this time, regardless of their personal feelings about its contents, Tad and Ricky had consumed so much of the punch that they lost interest in making any more, so the task fell to Willie and me. This third bowl was not nearly as refined, but the ingredients were essentially the same, except we added some of Gena Grigg's tranquilizers from the shelf above the sink. According to those gathered, our punch was the best.

Toward the end of the evening, perhaps a logical result of the tranquilizers in our concoction, someone requested coffee. Gena didn't have any, so Willie and I set out to find some.

Headed toward the main street, we took a short cut through the Chase Hotel, directly behind the Grigg house. While walking through the building, we saw a waiter leave a large coffee service tray on a stand in the hallway as he entered someone's room.

Timing is everything! As soon as the waiter was out of sight, we grabbed the tray and made a hasty, albeit very careful retreat with our prize, retracing our steps back to the Grigg house.

We proudly presented our booty, which was complete with sugar, cream, dishes and silverware, and served it to our stupefied friends. Gena, of course, was in no condition to notice the labels on the dishes or the monograms on the linen. Still under the influence of our famous punch, she was effusive in her praise for our producing such a professional coffee service.

The next day, after we had returned to Ocean Beach, Gena discovered where the coffee service came from and was mortified. It was not until many years later that she stopped checking everything we brought into her home.

Dick Ryan, 1948

Chapter 11

Remembering Dick Ryan

The Ryan family lived on top of the hill that overlooks Ocean Beach. Dick, Peggy, older son Ricky "with ears" and Tommy, the baby, came to the beach every day in the summer. Dick, with his movie-star good looks, had been a lifeguard. He also played the saxophone and after the war was leader of his own Dick Ryan Band, at the time the most popular group in San Diego. Peggy, who also looked like a movie star, worked nights as a cocktail waitress at Bali Ha'i, a restaurant on Shelter Island. She was a great cook, and I was fortunate to be invited to dinner often, because for some reason the boys would eat better when I was there.

Ricky and Tommy with author (back) 1956

In those days, Bali Ha'i had entertainment, provided by a Hawaiian orchestra and island dancers. During the day, most of the Hawaiian entertainers hung out on the sand at Ocean Beach. I often met Dick where his band was playing, and after his gig we would go to the Bali Ha'i to meet Peggy and then out to breakfast.

One Saturday we arrived about two in the morning, just as

the Bali Ha'i was closing. Peggy was all jittery and excited because Frank Sinatra had been there and invited all the employees to his yacht, docked in a nearby marina. Peggy invited Dick and me to join them, but only if we promised to behave. I am sure her comment was primarily for my benefit, but we both swore to be good. So off we went, intrigued with the idea of partying with Frank Sinatra.

As soon as we were aboard Sinatra's boat, Dick and I toured the extravagant floating party house, now packed with party-goers. We climbed up to the flying bridge and looked down at the dock on the starboard side, where the party had overflowed. As Dick and I surveyed the scene, I asked if he thought we could clear the boat and the dock if we dove from where we were standing on the bridge. He thought we could and promised to try, so long as I went first. So I removed my shoes and off I went with Dick behind me, flying over the revelers. We landed with quite a splash, drenching everyone near the outside of the dock. Peggy was so embarrassed she immediately left the party and went home, leaving us to walk the three miles back to their house in the darkness of early morning.

Another notable Saturday night adventure occurred when I was dating Robin Grigg. We went to see Dick and his band perform at Rosie's, in Ocean Beach. We closed down the joint and, because it was a beautiful night, decided to go to the beach, where the three of us continued drinking until sunrise. I don't remember who suggested it, but we then decided to go surfing at Windansea in La Jolla. We retrieved our boards from the lifeguard station and drove to La Jolla, arriving just as it was getting light.

Windansea is a famous California surf spot with a reef break at the foot of Nautilus Street. It has an exceptionally fast takeoff. I was first into the water and immediately caught a wave and surfed in toward shore. As I was paddling out for the next one, I saw Dick take off, fall on his back and shoot across the shoulder of the wave. His board went the other direction. Once Dick completed the arduous task of collecting his board, he retreated to the beach and didn't come out again.

At about the same time, Robin and I took off on a wave to the left. She fell, and one end of her board smacked her on the butt. I saw her just floating in the water, so I paddled over to check. She was stunned by the force of the blow, so I pulled her out of the water and onto my board. We paddled back to the beach together, and I retrieved her board. It was obviously time to follow Dick's example and quit for the day. Even now, after all the intervening years, Robin still sports a dent in her butt where the board hit her.

On another occasion, Robin, Bill Sampson, a lifeguard friend from Santa Monica and Stanford University law student, and a bunch of us from Ocean Beach drove to Baja to dive for lobster. In those days, you could buy cherry bombs in Mexico. So, while he was there, Sampson, who had this thing for explosives, purchased a bag full.

Dick and his band were playing a gig at the Hideaway in Hillcrest, on Fifth Street between University and Washington. Owned by Frank Harris, the Hideaway was the "in spot" at the time. We returned from Baja in the late afternoon and decided to finish our little vacation there.

We arrived late in the evening, when the Hideaway was packed and the dance floor was jammed with sweaty, inebriated bodies. Sampson had put a bunch of the Baja cherry bombs in his pocket, and during the course of the evening, with his judgment affected by an abundant consumption of alcohol, decided to set off a few.

The Hideaway was decorated with tall planter boxes that surrounded the dance floor and provided all the enticement Sampson needed. He put a cherry bomb with a delayed fuse into each planter. Then we all stood back and waited for the results. Sampson did a good job, and the explosions were perfect, as one planter after another went off, throwing flowers and plants and peet moss all over the floor, the walls and even the ceiling.

Amid the shrieks and stampede from the dance floor, Frank wasted no time in throwing us out, admonishing us never to return. Dick, who was busy minding his own business and playing his music, was madder than hell that he had been upstaged.

Years later, in the early seventies, Dick died during a failed heart transplant operation. Ricky, Tommy, Mouse and I put his ashes in the Pacific at the foot of Osprey Street. I still think of him often, and I miss his friendship and his music.

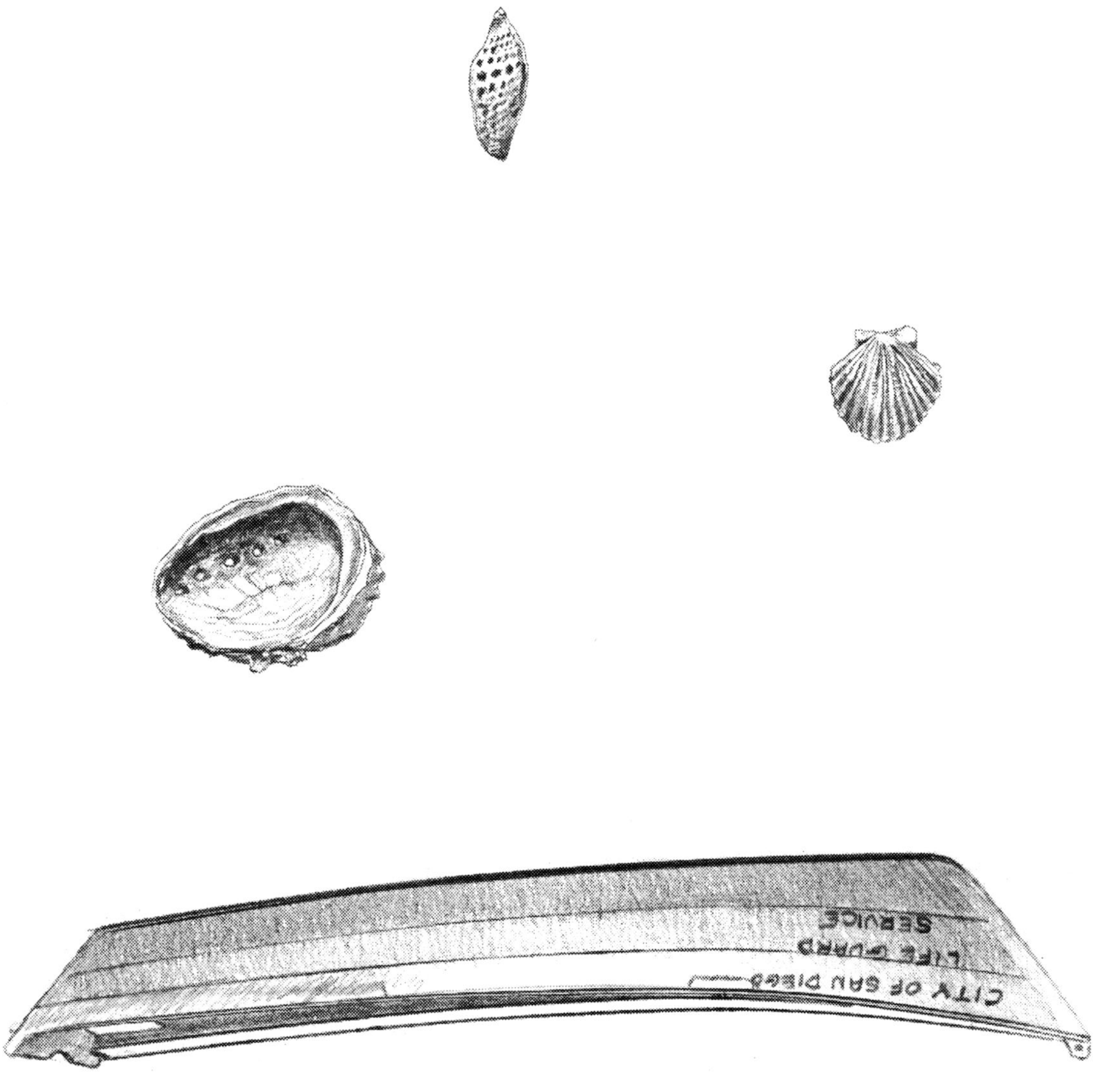

Chapter 12

May Britt

One summer my friend, Bill Sampson, introduced me to the exciting Swedish movie star, May (pronounced Mai) Britt. Bill was dating her sister, and the three of them were spending the weekend at Ocean Beach.

May was the most striking woman I had ever met and a knockout in her two-piece swimsuit, as she was lithe, blond and drop-dead beautiful. She was the kind of girl that provoked the instant urge to merge. I was immediately smitten and, even better, she seemed to like me! I began having visions of paradise, and her attentions immediately increased my status on the beach. Even Mouse was impressed.

To further my cause with May, I decided to take her out in the lifeguard dory to ride the waves. Because the boat is twenty feet long and made of wood, it is big and heavy and really needs a two-person crew, as it is difficult to manage. Also because of its size and weight, surfing the dory is difficult and requires great skill which, at the moment, I believed I possessed. Regardless, I took May out alone.

She sat in the bow while I rowed from the stern, and we plowed out through the waves without incident. Outside the break, in calm water, I continued rowing and showed May how to turn the boat and how to work it with the ocean currents and swells. Then I demonstrated how the dory could be used to rescue a swimmer, showing off my best professional attitude and skills.

After I thought I had made enough of an impression, I turned the dory toward shore, got in the lineup, and waited for a small wave so we could surf the boat back into the beach. It was my luck that at that very moment a large set came in, hoisting us on a much larger swell than I had anticipated. We went flying down the face of the wave when the dory suddenly broached, and over we went. We both were flung out of the boat and into the water. May was hit hard on the head by one of the oars, the crewless dory was being washed ashore, and now I had a real rescue on my hands. I swam to where May was struggling in the surf and pulled her into shallow water so she could stand.

And somehow I knew. At the instant the dory overturned, my fantasy about having a relationship with this gorgeous creature abruptly ended.

With her sister and my friend Bill, May left the beach early, returning to Los Angeles to recover from her ordeal. I knew I would never see her again. But I could watch her movies and fantasize about what might have been had I not been responsible for her being thrown out of the lifeguard rescue boat that one summer day.

After all is said and done,
there is a lot more said than done.
(Mark Twain)

Brendan McCullan

Chapter 13

Makapuu Mooks

He was a lifeguard in Laguna Beach and one of the most interesting characters I ever knew. He was a large man with a large heart and an even larger sense of humor. His real name was Brendan Mclland. But he was called, depending on where you were, either “Hevs” or “Makapuu Mooks.” He got the name Hevs because of his stature and the other name, I am told, because of a body surfing incident in Hawaii.

Makapuu Point is a famous body surfing spot on the southwest corner of the Island of Oahu. The waves come from the south, hit the point and shoulder hard to the left, around a coral reef. Once, on a big day at Makapuu, Hevs took off and didn’t go left. Thus he body surfed to shore across the sharp coral. When he finally landed, his fins had been ripped off, and his entire body was cut, courtesy of the coral reef. Bloodied but undaunted, he went right back out and did the same thing. Again he went right, repeating his bloody feat. This would have killed an ordinary surfer, but not Hevs. Out into the break again. But this time he had gotten the message. He took off on a wave, kicked powerfully to the left and made it in without any more damage. From then on in the Islands, he was known as, “Makapuu Mooks.”

To most Southern California beach goers in the fifties, Hevs was remarkable. The stories about his life are many and legendary, enough for an entire book. My two favorites follow.

In Laguna Beach where Hevs grew up, he accumulated quite a following through the years. In August 1957 at a Laguna Beach surf contest at Brooks Street, Hevs announced he was despondent over a love gone sour and soon, on a particular

Sunday, planned to commit suicide in front of the beach crowd. At one in the afternoon, he would dive out of an airplane flying just offshore at an altitude of only two hundred feet.

On the appointed day, a large number of curious onlookers gathered on the beach to witness this event. Precisely at the appointed time, a small, high-wing craft flew over, in front of the beach. To the horror of the crowd, a body came hurtling out of the plane, hit the water near the kelp bed just offshore and sank. The collected crowd gasped in horror, and the lifeguards started out to get the body. As all this was going on, Hevs, who had been hiding in the kelp where the body landed, washed ashore on a wave and triumphantly greeted the crowd. Neither the lifeguards nor the local police were amused.

The second of my favorite "Hev" stories was the time the local city fathers were trying to close access to Salt Beach in Laguna Beach, an action that was violently opposed by the beach goers. A public meeting was scheduled to address the issue, and Hevs was chosen to speak for the opposition. What began as a rowdy meeting deteriorated to ugly, and Hevs was the last speaker. He wasn't making much progress with the governing body, so when he finished his pitch, Hevs directed closing remarks to his principal antagonist by pointing a very large index finger at him, declaring, "And you, sir, are a charlatan, a mountebank and a porch climber!" Which brought the assembled group to its feet with a resounding cheer. The meeting ended with the furniture broken to pieces in the closing riot.

And access to Salt Beach remained open.

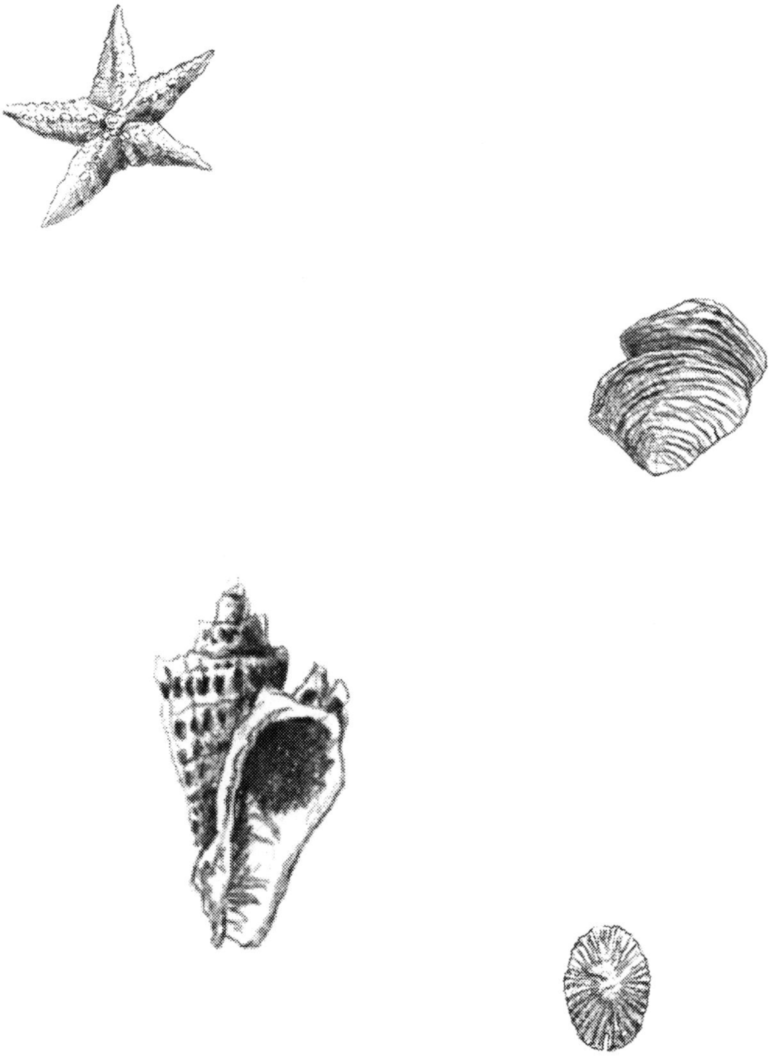

Chapter 14

Swim in Front of the Green Flag!

It was a hot Tuesday in October, the kind of stuffy, windless day typical of early autumn in Southern California. The tide was low, the surf was about three feet, and the beach was quiet, as we were three weeks into the school year. I stuck the green flag into the sand, designating the safe swimming area in front of the tower. I posted the red flag, designating the unsafe swimming area, about one hundred yards to the south, at the foot of Newport Avenue.

About one in the afternoon, a group of swimmers splashed into the water directly in front of the red flag. They were all pale-skinned, a tip-off to any lifeguard that these were not beach people. Perhaps they also were color-blind?

So I climbed down from the tower, got into the jeep and drove south along the beach. I began signaling the errant swimmers with my whistle. They did not respond. I blew longer and louder blasts on the whistle. Nothing happened.

Finally, hopping mad at being ignored, I jumped out of the jeep and stormed across the beach into the water. Wading through the waist-deep surf, I got to the nearest person in the group, grabbed him by the arm, turned him around and shouted in his face, "Didn't you hear me?" He motioned with his hands to his ears and mouth. I understood his communication. Mortified, I realized that he, and all the others, were deaf.

I was so embarrassed I just wanted to drown myself.

Instead, I pointed him toward shore and then went to every person in the group, directing them all to the beach. Once they were assembled out of the water, I led them to the green flag area and pointed and motioned until they understood that this was a safe place to swim.

They spent the rest of the afternoon happily splashing and swimming in front of the green flag, while I kept a comfortable watch over them. Late in the day, as they were getting ready to leave, they all came to the tower and thanked me in sign language.

Goddamn an eye witness,
he always spoils a good story
(Colonel Crisp)

Chapter 15

Rescues and Recoveries

WE SHOULD HAVE CLOSED THE BEACH

In August 1955, the U.S. Army Corps of Engineers was dredging the Mission Bay Channel. As the dredge worked toward the outside end of the jetty, it pumped sand through huge pipes onto Ocean Beach, all the way from the Silver Spray Hotel at the north end of the beach to the jetty on the south. This sand fill effectively widened the beach and created a four- to five-foot drop-off where the ocean met the shore

Everything went fine during the dredging process until one Saturday in late August when a large swell hit the west coast. Early in the day, the tide was exceptionally high, and the break was right at the shoreline. When the ten- to twelve-foot breakers hit the new, steep drop-off created by the accumulation of fill sand, they broke straight down with tremendous force, as there was nowhere for the energy of the wave to dissipate.

It was an unusually hot day, so the beach was already crowded. The combination of the new drop-off created by the dredged sand and the huge waves breaking directly onshore created deadly conditions. Those of us on duty discussed the situation and, for reasons of public safety, decided to clear the beach. But our attempts to do so resulted in a wave of protest, and someone even called lifeguard headquarters to complain. The complaint was obviously heard, as Captain Hardy phoned to reverse our decision. He ordered me to open the beach.

By then, the tide had started to recede. The waves were still large, and they were breaking several yards offshore, but conditions were hardly less dangerous. So, with six guards on duty, we confined the swimming area as much as possible, and each guard stood at water's edge with a rescue buoy strapped to his waist, ready to hit the water in an instant. We were in and out all day, pulling swimmers out of swift rip currents and crushing surf.

Although we took special precautions and made many rescues, we made one too few. Late in the afternoon, some of the kids who had been at the beach all day came to where I was standing at the edge of the drop-off and crowded around to report one of their buddies missing. I notified the other guards, and we implemented a water and beach search, but without success. The missing boy could not be found.

Several days later, someone found the body of a teenage boy washed ashore. The missing friend. His neck was broken, probably from being "planted" by one of the huge waves that had been breaking at the shoreline drop-off on Saturday.

I have always wished we had been allowed to close the beach that day.

THE MINISTER'S BOXER

At the foot of Point Loma Avenue, on the ocean side of the street, the houses give way in deference to the steep cliffs. Across the street is a Lutheran church, "Saint Peter's by the Sea." During the fifties, the church pastor had a beautiful boxer dog that played along these cliffs, safely above the surf that pounded the rocks below.

One rainy, windy winter day, I received a call from lifeguard headquarters that someone was in trouble at the foot of Point Loma Avenue. Doug Smith and I set out in the lifeguard cliff rig, an orange pickup truck with a boom that protruded over the back and a pulley with which someone could be raised or lowered over a cliff. When we arrived on the scene, an expectant crowd had gathered. As we exited the truck and looked over the edge of the cliff, we anticipated an injured person lying somewhere below. To our surprise, we were wrong. It was the pastor's boxer that was the object of all the fuss. The dog had been playing along the edge of the cliff when he apparently slipped and fell toward the water. His fall was interrupted by a protruding ledge where he was now trapped, about twenty feet below where we stood.

Because of the dog's position, it was impossible to get the cliff rig close enough to use. Instead, I climbed down the cliff into the water and swam to the ledge where the dog was trapped. He was wet, cold and very happy to see me. Over the sound of the rain, wind and surf, I yelled to Doug, who was watching from above, to tie himself to the guard rail next to the street, climb down, and I would hand him the dog. We tried, but the cliff was too muddy and slippery to make the rescue that way. So, hand-over-hand, Doug lowered a line, which I fastened around the dog. Doug then pulled him up, as the dog tried to help, scrambling to gain a foothold on the steep, muddy surface.

After finally getting the dog to safety, I climbed down to the water and swam to a small beach from where I could climb back up the cliffs. By this time, the minister had taken his dog home, the crowd had dispersed, and only Doug waited at the top.

A photographer had been on the cliffs during the entire ordeal and got a picture of me trying to hand the dog to Doug through the rain and sea spray. The photograph supposedly ran on the front page of the New York Times, although I never saw it.

The minister was very appreciative and thereafter, I was told, did a lot of praying for the welfare of the lifeguards.

A CAVE RESCUE

I knew when I used an offering of fresh lobster to con the telephone man into running an extension line from the lifeguard tower across the driveway to the "cubby hole" where I lived, that Captain Hardy would be suspicious of my explanation that it was to answer emergency calls at night. But, for fear of disrupting our established routine of abalone sandwich lunches, he just told me not to make any long distance calls.

As fate would have it, a week later my con job became reality. About four o'clock one cold, stormy, rainy winter morning, I received a phone call from Gus Petro, working the midnight-to-eight shift at the Channel Lifeguard Station. Gus said a power boat had gone aground along the cliffs on the ocean side of Point Loma, where the surf was huge and winds were blowing at about

40 knots. Gus picked me up at the Ocean Beach station, and together we drove out to the point.

We were met by the Navy fire department truck that served the Naval Electronics Laboratory, complete with a contingent of firemen, all fully dressed in their fire-fighting gear. I took one look and hoped they didn't intend to get into the water, weighted down with all their clothes and equipment. But that incident had already occurred.

The cliffs that lead down to the churning water were wet and slippery, and one of the firefighters had already fallen. As I feared, he was struggling in the water, unable to rescue himself. Our first task, then, was to rescue the fire-fighter, incapacitated by the weight if his clothing and equipment and boots, and now all full of water. Gus and I jumped into the water with a line and tied it to the helpless man. His buddies hauled him up from above while we pushed from below.

Then we turned our attention to our real task, to rescue the shipwrecked crew from the power boat. We couldn't see the capsized boat, but we could hear voices yelling from a cave in the cliffs, where the crashing surf blocked the mouth of the cave. Gus and I conferred, and I decided to jump in first and try to gain entrance to the cave. At the first lull in the pounding waves, I jumped from the cliff and bodysurfed right into the cave, where five wet, tired, injured and frightened boaters were waiting, shivering. All were cut, bleeding and in shock, and two of the three women had broken bones.

As I entered the cave, I remember one woman yelling, “Thank God, we’re saved!” I didn’t say anything, but I thought to myself, “Not yet, sister, not yet.” After seeing the serious condition of the five people inside, I realized their injuries would prevent any of them from getting out the same way they had gotten in.

So I explored further into the cave and found a second outlet to the ocean. This one was protected from the south by a reef and was out of line of the menacing surf. A large, flat rock lay strategically within the protected area. So I exited through this “back door” and yelled over the noise of the surf and wind and rain for Gus to come down and help. He climbed and slid through the mud down to the water’s edge where he could swim to this protected entrance.

We tried to comfort the injured people, assured them they would be all right and prepared them for the task ahead. When we had tended to everyone as best we could, I swam out and climbed back up the cliff to confer with the rescue workers. We decided the best way to get the victims to safety would be with a helicopter.

So back I went, slithering down the cliff, into the water and swimming back to the cave entrance to rejoin Gus and our shipwreck survivors and inform them of the plan. In those days, because none of the lifeguards had wetsuits, Gus and I were clad only in our lifeguard trunks. Although we were not injured, we were as cold and uncomfortable as the others. Hypothermia was playing favorites with nobody.

Soon a Navy helicopter arrived, and a basket was lowered onto our flat rescue rock. One by one, Gus and I got our charges out to the rock, put them into the basket, strapped them securely, and watched as they were lifted to the top of the cliffs above. Then Gus went up in the basket. When it was finally my turn, before I could get settled, the winch on the line jammed, just as a big wave hit. The pilot, fearing I might otherwise be smashed against the rocks, just took off. Up I went, dangling from the basket.

I hung on until the pilot set me down on firm ground. There was no further incident or injury, but Gus and I were covered with cuts and scratches.

Strangely, we never had any word from the people we rescued. I have always wondered why. But Captain Hardy was proud of us! Gus and I each received three days off with pay, the first Ocean Beach lifeguards to earn such a reward.

THE BOAT AT CORONADO STREET

On a stormy winter day, a thirty-foot motor yacht, headed to San Diego Bay from Mission Bay, lost power off Coronado and was blown into the surf line. The lifeguard station received a call that the boat was in trouble. With Don Mellon, who was working with me that day, we grabbed a couple of rescue buoys and a pair of fins and headed to the beach nearest the disaster in the lifeguard jeep. We arrived just in time to see a large wave overturn the boat and throw its two passengers, a middle-aged couple, into the water.

At that time of year, the water temperature was about fifty-five degrees, as it was the era before wetsuits. We would do our job in just our swim trunks.

As we were climbing down the cliffs, I sarcastically asked Don if he wanted one of my fins. When he said, "Yes," I pretended not to hear, because when I had stopped long enough to grab mine, he had scoffed and insulted my swimming talents. Now he could show me his.

As we headed into the surf a Coast Guard helicopter arrived and lowered a sling into the water. The man got in the sling with his legs wrapped around his wife's waist. Because of the uncertainty of his hold on her, the helicopter began dragging them through the water toward shore. When we got to them the man let go of his wife losing his pants in the process.

The wife had drowned. So we started to carry the body to shore. But the helicopter continued to hover, just overhead, the updraft from the rotor blades creating its own surf, making it almost impossible for us to get a breath without inhaling a lung full of spray. Don tried to wave them off, but the helicopter just stayed close. Too close. We struggled against the turbulence created as the helicopter followed us and managed to get the woman's body into shore. The husband survived.

That experience was as close as I ever came to believing that I might actually drown. And it was the last time that Don ever went out on a rescue at the cliffs without his fins. The event made the wire service and got national attention.

BODY SEARCH AT SAN QUINTIN

San Quintin is a large coastal farming community on the Pacific side of the Baja Peninsula, about two hundred miles south of Tijuana, Mexico. In the fifties, the paved road ran south as far as San Vicente, but that was about fifty miles short of San Quintin.

San Quintin Bay was a favorite spot for duck hunters, as it was a huge, U-shaped body of water, several miles across. And it was shallow, so a steady wind was enough to create rough and dangerous seas. Beneath the shallow water, the shifting sands created incised channels, about eight to ten feet deep, along the ocean floor.

The bay had attracted an older couple who, with two Mexican guides, had been out hunting ducks. They were in the seaward arm of the bay, known as "False Bay," when the afternoon wind came up, creating turbulent conditions that flipped their boat. All four aboard drowned in the incident. The wife's body surfaced, but days later, the three others were still missing.

A few days later, the family of the drowned couple hired my pal Willie to search for the body of the husband. In turn, Willie asked me to partner on the dive, and the next day we were flown in a small, single-engine plane to the airstrip at the Santa Maria Sky Ranch at San Quintin. The resort had been established by crooner Bing Crosby in the forties but was now run by an Ocean Beach businessman, Bob Zinghim. We arrived late in the afternoon, by then too windy and too late to dive. So we availed ourselves of the local seafood and cerveza and practiced our Spanish.

The next morning, we loaded our diving gear and motored out into the bay in two Mexican pangas, which were small, open-water boats equipped with undersized outboard motors. As we headed out to False Bay, we were skeptical of ever accomplishing our goal of locating the drowned man. Several days and numerous tide changes had passed since the disaster, and the body could be anywhere. The tide was going out as our boat approached the area where it was believed the victims went down. So we decided to start our search from the north end of the bay, as it would be more efficient to swim with, rather than

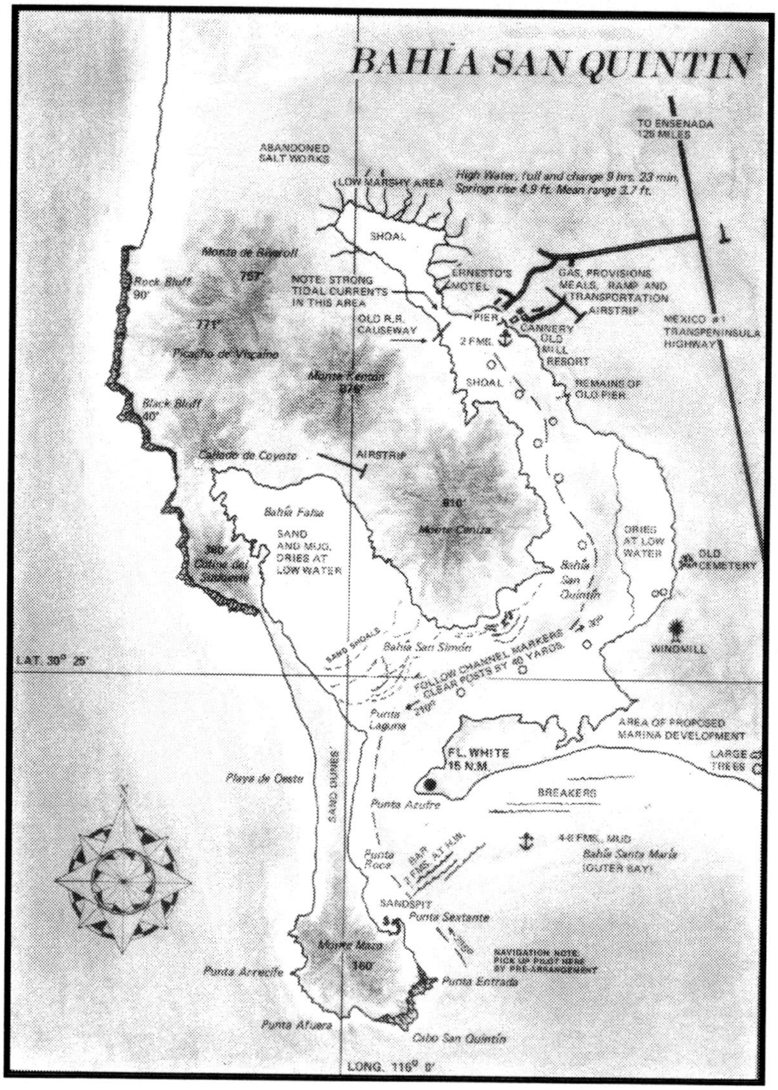

San Quintin Bay, 1956
©SEA Publications

against, the outflowing tide.

The area of San Quintin Bay where the tragedy occurred was especially shallow, with a heavily channeled bottom. So Willie and I decided we each would take a different channel. I went down one while Willie followed another. As I drifted along on the outgoing tide, I noticed the ocean bottom was full of worm rocks — large, porous boulders full of holes, that were themselves full of lobsters. It was difficult not to just grab some "bugs," but I was getting paid to search for a body, and I knew Willie would be pissed if I started filling the pangas with lobster. So I just looked longingly at the lobsters while I drifted with the tide and searched for the drowned man.

After about thirty minutes under water, and just as my tank was running out of air, I drifted over a large dark form. Startled, I stopped. It was a human body. It was also just blind luck. I grabbed the drowned man by the arm, hauled him to the surface, spit out my regulator and yelled to our guides in the pongas. They managed to lift the body over the side and into the boat. It was the husband.

I wanted to keep diving and bring in some of the lobster, so abundant on the ocean floor. The water was so shallow, I could just free dive. But Willie thought it would be in bad taste, so we returned to Sky Ranch.

The two Mexican guides were still missing, but Willie and I were out of air, and there was no place in San Quintin to get our tanks filled. So our employers decided it was time to take us home.

All the way back, I kept thinking of those lobsters. I was disappointed at not being able to bring some home. Then I reminded myself of the real purpose of our trip. I had, though, extended the range of my diving experience, as it was the first time I had been diving that far down the Pacific side of the Baja peninsula.

THE BOAT OFF THE SOUTH MISSION BAY JETTY

One clear, sunny day in early December 1957, the surf was huge and the water was its customary winter temperature, a cold 55 degrees, when a small boat exited the Mission Bay Channel and headed south toward Ocean Beach. I was in the tower and watched with anticipation as the boat moved into the lineup, directly in the path of a big set of fifteen-foot waves. The second wave in the set threw the boat into the air, where it overturned, dumping its two passengers into the foam.

I yelled to Doug Smith, who was working with me that day, to grab his fins and get the jeep running. I climbed down from the tower, grabbed my own fins and yelled for Doug to, “Hit it!” as I jumped into the jeep and we headed south toward the jetty, about three-quarters of a mile away.

The surf was so big it was not possible to swim straight out from the beach, so we ran out onto the jetty, jumped into the water and from there swam toward the overturned craft. When we got to the boat, with the surf breaking over it, I saw one man was trapped underneath. I managed to get him out, but he was already dead. Doug searched unsuccessfully for the other man, who wasn’t found until several days later when is body washed ashore.

Some weeks after the mishap, the families of both men came to the beach for a memorial service near where the tragedy occurred. It was then we learned that neither man could swim and that this had been their first boat. During the ceremony I was reminded of the words of Titihuti, Marquesans Princess, who observed at a parting of a dear friend: "We come we do not know whence, and we go, we do not know where. Only the sea endures, and it does not remember." (White Shadows in the South Seas, p. 446, Frederick O'Brien, 1920)

A BODY ON THE BEACH AT LADERA

Where Sunset Cliffs Boulevard ends, you turn left, and that's Ladera Street, perched high above the ocean. One day we received a call reporting a landslide of the cliffs below Ladera Street. The caller said that someone was on the beach below when the slide occurred. Mouse and I were working that day, so we went Code 3 (red light and siren), racing the lifeguard truck along Sunset Cliffs Boulevard to the slide area. In those days, to get to the beach below Ladera Street, you had to climb down the rocks just south of Hill Street and go up to Ladera, or go all the way to base of the cliffs called "garbage" and backtrack to Ladera.

Since getting to the beach was easier and shorter by going down the rocks near Hill Street, we chose that route. The tide was out, so we ran north to the slide. When we arrived, we discovered that the initial report was true and we were too late to do any good;

a sunbather lying under the cliff had been killed by the cave-in.

By now the fire department also had arrived, drawing a curious crowd of onlookers to the cliffs at Ladera Street, high above the tragedy. I yelled at the firemen and told them we had a dead person and needed a basket. When they yelled back something about Mouse and me carrying the body back up the cliff, I responded with as much profanity as I could remember learning from my Navy pals. The firemen finally agreed.

We waited and finally saw the telescoping boom protrude over the cliffs, lowering the basket and body bag. As the basket was on its way down, I suggested to Mouse that he get in the bag and when they got him up to the street above the cliffs he could start yelling, "I'm alive! I'm alive!" Exercising excellent judgment, Mouse refused.

However, since my judgment was frequently flawed, I got into the bag any way, and Mouse secured it to the basket, then hollered for the firemen to haul me up. When I felt the basket on the ground, I begin to yell and kick from inside the body bag. I guess it scared the shit out of the firemen, but mostly they were just pissed. Now they had to again go through the entire routine to haul up the real body.

THE MARINES!

Near the end of the summer of 1959, I retired from the lifeguards to go to law school, even though I was in line to become the next lifeguard lieutenant. I still lived at the beach, about a block from the lifeguard station and paid the bills by working as a commercial diver. And my wife was VERY pregnant.

As I returned from classes one afternoon, about the middle of October 1960, I noted huge surf and, just north of the lifeguard tower, a rip current. I knew it had created a deep hole.

During that time of year, the off season, only two guards were stationed at Ocean Beach -- on this particular day, Billy Norton and Mike Rogers. As I parked my car, I noticed the lifeguard jeep down by the water, but no lifeguards near it. Out of habit, I scanned the beach. That's when I saw them -- Billy and Mike, in the water, each with a rescue buoy, and holding three young men afloat. I later learned that the three men were marine recruits from the Midwest, taking their first swim in the Pacific Ocean.

As I watched, I could see that neither guard was making any headway toward the beach. As soon as one got into the surf line, he was washed into the hole and then pushed into the rip, with the result that all five men were being swept in a continuous circle.

I went into the station and called lifeguard headquarters for help, then headed down the beach toward the jeep. I peeled off my shirt and shoes, grabbed the rescue line that was attached to the jeep on a big spool, and started out into the water, toward the struggling men. I should have taken off my long pants, but I had nothing on underneath, and I was too modest to go in the buff.

When I got near the five men, I yelled for Billy to swim over and attach his rescue buoy to the line from the jeep. To accomplish this, he transferred all three Marines to Mike's buoy.

Then he swam toward me to snap onto the jeep line. I assumed he would attach his buoy to the line, then swim it back to the Marines while I swam to the beach and reeled them all in.

But it didn't quite work that way. When Billy got to me and I handed him the line, he just dropped it, exhausted. So I took his buoy, he swam to shore, and I swam out to Mike, still struggling with the three Marines. By this time Mike also was exhausted, so he gave me his buoy, with the Marines, and swam to shore. Well, I and the three Marines and two rescue buoys rolled around in the hole for what seemed like forever, and I thought we all might drown. Finally I decided to at least save myself. Onshore, fatherhood was imminent. Somehow I finally gained a foothold and was able to pull the four of us out of the hole and parallel to shore until we got out of the rip. About this time, lifeguards from the southern section arrived and helped get us all into the beach.

I really felt good about that rescue, but my wife was madder than hell that I had risked my life when she was pregnant. After all, I wasn't even a lifeguard anymore. I guess it would have been all right if she hadn't been so close to motherhood.

AN EXCEPTIONALLY WELL-ENDOWED LADY IN A BIKINI

It was late summer, and it was the kind of oppressive heat that happens along the coast about four weeks of every year, when even the air is too hot to muster the energy to move. The surf was up, with a drag to the south toward the rocks and the Sunset Cliffs surfing area. We had stationed the dory on the sand next to the water in front of the rip, anticipating its use. Among the throng of beach-goers was a beautiful, exceptionally well-endowed woman wearing a provocative two-piece swimsuit, and her boyfriend, who was not as beautiful.

At about three in the afternoon, the two were cooling themselves in the water when they were caught up in the rip and pulled away from the beach by the current. Doug Smith and I saw them being dragged out to sea, so we launched the dory into the surf and made our way out to them. As we rowed near the couple, I yelled for the woman to give me her hand. It was my intent to pull her over the rail and into the dory between Doug and me. Then we would pull in the boyfriend. Just as we reached for her, though, a series of events created a crisis. First, a huge set of waves appeared outside, threatening to overturn us unless we hurried, which we did. But as soon as I grabbed the woman's arm to pull her into the boat, the halter top of her swimsuit fell to her waist. We didn't mind, but the boyfriend did. The instant he noticed she was topless, he grabbed her by the waist to keep us from lifting her into the dory, as her breasts were now fully exposed.

The wave set, however, was fast approaching and, because of its size, threatened to capsize the dory. I was yelling at the boyfriend to let go of the woman so we could get her into the boat and to safety. The boyfriend, however, kept fighting to preserve his girlfriend's (or his) dignity, jeopardizing all of us in the process.

It was obvious that the boyfriend was not going to release

his hold. We had to do something, or the situation would be far more catastrophic than one of mere exposure. So I made a command decision to take drastic action. I grabbed an oar, leaned out over the side of the boat and hit the boyfriend on the head. Stunned, he loosened his grip on the woman, and we were able to pull her into the dory just in time to avoid being capsized. We then hurriedly rowed out past the waves to the safety of calmer water so we could set up the boat and the three of us for a safe trip to shore.

We positioned ourselves in the dory and, with our passenger seated in the middle and hanging on to the sides, we rowed over the next wave and surfed the boat into the beach without incident. Once in shallow water, we helped the woman climb out and watched until she was safely ashore. Then we went back to retrieve the angry boyfriend. When we were all safely on dry land, the woman expressed her gratitude, but her boyfriend was still not happy. Not only had we hit him on the head and rendered him helpless, but we had seen his girlfriend's breasts. As lifeguards, we wondered at his priorities. But, thankfully, he was no longer our problem.

Chapter 16

Mouse and the Great White Shark

Mouse was one of the kindest persons and one of the best lifeguards I ever worked with. His real name was James Robb, but he had always been called "Mouse" because of his diminutive size.

As a kid in the late forties, Mouse started surfing on a board made of redwood and oak. Called a plank, the board was three times his length and twice his body weight. Of necessity, like most surfers who learned to surf without a leash, Mouse also became a strong swimmer, body surfer and diver.

He was then, and is today, one of the best surfers in the Ocean Beach-Sunset Cliffs area, or anywhere else, for that matter. Always light, muscular and strong of heart, he still lives and surfs in the same area. And he has probably saved more lives over the past forty years than any other person around these waters.

Mouse worked as a lifeguard in the summers of 1955 and 1956. In the fifties, Ocean Beach used a surf dory. Most of the other beaches that had dories seldom used them for rescues. At these beaches, when someone was in trouble in the water, it was easier and faster for the lifeguards to just swim out with the rescue buoy. But at Ocean Beach, because of the ever-present rip currents, and because it was fun, we saved many a swimmer with our dory. We also used it for crowd control when there was a strong onshore wind.

The dory was big and heavy, about twenty feet long, and

required two lifeguards to maneuver it. The bow man would row from a seated position, facing the back of the boat. The stern man would row while standing, facing the front and was the "captain." In the two summers Mouse worked as an Ocean Beach lifeguard, he was my favorite dory partner, which leads to this story.

Early in the morning of June 15, 1959, in the ocean off Alligator Rock, at La Jolla Cove, a sailor severely cut his foot and bled profusely into the water. Early in the afternoon of the same day, a great white shark gobbled up skin diver Robert Pamperin at that same spot. At the time, because I was the official diver for the lifeguard service, I was sent to look for any remains of the skin diver's body. I called a couple of friends to join me, Jon Lindberg, a former Navy UDT officer and son of aviator Charles Lindberg, and Willie Meyers, a former first class Navy hard hat diver. The three of us searched the ocean bottom until dark, but without success. It was pretty scary, looking for human body parts, all the while anticipating the shark returning for dessert.

The media was immediately abuzz with the story, and there was speculation the death had been staged to collect a large life insurance policy. I spoke to Pamperin's diving partner, Gerald Fehrer, at the scene, and I am convinced the event happened just the way it was reported.

Anyway, that is background for the subsequent theatrics at Ocean Beach several weeks later. It was a bright, sunny Sunday. The beach was crowded, the water was warm, and the surf was more than decent.

About two in the afternoon, I was taking my turn in the portable tower near the water when I spotted what looked like a shark fin about one-hundred-fifty yards offshore, directly out from the bathing area. Jon Kowel, a lifeguard lieutenant who was very excitable and given to making impulsive decisions, had just arrived in his truck. I called him up into the tower and asked him to take a look.

After just one quick glance at the water, Jon jumped down from the tower, got into his truck, turned on the red light and siren, and began driving up and down the beach screaming, "Shark!" over his public address system and yelling for bathers to get out of the water. Meanwhile, Mouse and Willie, who were on beach duty, volunteered to go with me in the dory to attack the "shark."

Example of dory used in "shark hunt"

Caught up in the hysteria of the moment, my two companions and I pulled the dory into the surf and jumped in, armed with an old, rusty, twenty-two rifle. We would "get the shark" and save the beach. Out we rowed, with myself as "captain" on the stern oars, Mouse on the bow oars, and Willie up front with the rifle. Hundreds of spectators gathered along the water's edge, watching this heroic crew going after what we believed to be the "great white shark" that had eaten Robert Pamperin several weeks earlier at La Jolla cove.

With a loaded boat and waves high enough to get the locals excited, it was a miracle we made it through the surf without capsizing. As we rowed closer and closer to our prey, the fin abruptly vanished! We stopped and looked. Perhaps the shark was under the dory! Then, a few yards away, it appeared again. We rowed toward it, very slowly and very, very carefully. Suddenly, the fin flopped sideways into the water — to reveal the belly of a seal happily sunning itself at the surface.

During the time it had taken us to row out to the "shark," the crowd on the beach continued to grow. Even the media was there, expecting to see a kill. "God," I thought after our disappointing discovery, "how will we explain this without being the laughing stock of the beach?"

The three of us managed a hurried conference in the dory and decided we had no choice but to make a show of it. We would not let on that our prey was only a seal.

In accordance with our plan, and being careful not to harm the seal, Willie began firing the rifle. Mouse rocked the dory, and I started beating the water with an oar. After several minutes of this spectacle, we triumphantly returned to shore, riding in on a wave for the benefit of the many cameras pointed in our direction. On the way in, we agreed to tell everyone it had been a shark, and we thought we killed it. Captain Hardy was quite proud of our heroic efforts, and the event became front-page news in San Diego.

Although many questioned why the dead "shark" never washed ashore, we stuck to our story. Until now.

Willie Meyers off Sunset Cliffs, 1955

Chapter 17

Sunset Cliffs

As you drive south on Sunset Cliffs Boulevard, the houses on the ocean side of the street end at Adair. From this point south is the area known as Sunset Cliffs. For several miles, the property is privately owned, then becomes government property all the way to the end of Point Loma and into San Diego Bay.

Directly west from the end of Sunset Cliffs Boulevard, at Ladera Street, and just offshore, lies a series of reefs the locals called "Garbage." The place got its name because, in the early days, there was a long chute where people dumped their garbage

John Callahan, Willie Meyers, Buzzy Bent, Bax, Bob Terry and George Raines

from the top of the cliff, the chute sending it down into the ocean. Everyone believed this garbage dump was the reason for the prolific breeding of lobsters and abalone in the area. They might have been right about the lobsters, but the abalone were there because of the huge offshore kelp beds.

Although the area was a favorite of local surfers and divers, it was dangerous for the novice, and even for seasoned scuba divers who were not adept at climbing down the steep, muddy cliff and entering the water through the rocks and surf. Many of the inexperienced got into real trouble here. The area was not guarded, so by the time someone called the lifeguards and we arrived on the scene, it was usually too late. The real "lifeguards" were the board surfers. I personally know that Mouse and other locals saved many lives during the time I worked as a lifeguard for the city. To this day, these surfers are still saving lives at Sunset Cliffs, quietly, without fuss or any special recognition.

In the fifties, on days the water was clear, it was common to dive for abalone and lobster and get your limit after less than an hour in the water. I remember many occasions when I brought up ten-to-twenty pound specimens. In those days, children didn't need fishing licenses to dive for abalone and lobster, so if I needed more than my one-person limit, I just took two or three kids down the cliffs with me and got their limits, too. Their mothers thought I was a great guy for providing several hours of free baby-sitting services. And the kids had fun, too, playing in the tide pools and getting grimy while I was out diving.

On one occasion when Fats and Ricky were still kids, I took them on one of these excursions. On the way home, walking along the cliffs, we passed a stretch of sand where a very healthy young lady lay on a blanket sunbathing, in the nude. Her head was toward the cliffs, her legs were apart with her feet pointed toward the ocean, and she had placed a big, floppy hat over her face.

It was low tide as the boys and I walked in the sand at water's edge. When we passed a few feet from where that sublime body lay, the kids' eyes became transfixed. So I said in a loud voice, "Boys, I know that lady because I would recognize her smile anywhere!" Well, the remark really pissed her off because she jumped to her feet and started yelling, "You dirty son-of-a-bitch!" and took off after us, wearing only her hat. Fats and Ricky were too young to understand what was happening, but when I started running away, they were right behind me. Now that both boys are grown, we sometimes have a good laugh over our incident with the "naked lady."

The Fish and Game warden usually on duty at Sunset Cliffs was Richard Inks, called "Uncle Dick" by everyone who knew him. Uncle Dick was about five-foot-ten and weighed about three hundred pounds. One afternoon, I was sitting with some friends under a big banyan tree at the cut in the cliff that provided access to the beach. At the base of the cliff trail was a drop-off of about ten feet. To get down, you could slide and jump to the beach. But to get up from the beach, you had to become a rock climber, using a rope attached to a big piece of pipe that had been driven into the cliff. After this, you walked up a narrow cut in the cliff that had been eroded by rain and foot traffic. This trail was about six to twelve feet deep and curved up the bank.

From under the tree, I saw Uncle Dick with his binoculars,

watching several kids diving for abalone in the shallow water offshore. Because the abalone were so plentiful, the young divers had already filled two gunny sacks. They were way over their limits!

Uncle Dick decided to make his way down to the beach to cite the young divers for their excessive catch, but his girth stopped him about a third of the way down the narrow trail.

Waiting for the kids to come up the bank with their abalone, Uncle Dick positioned himself just above the impassable spot. As the boys came around the turn, Uncle Dick stepped out, flashed his badge and said, “I’ve got you little shits now!” The first culprit in line gave him the finger, then they all turned and raced to the beach below. Uncle Dick was helpless to pursue as they ran up the beach and were gone.

Everyone in my group who was observing this remarkable scene was laughing so hard that Uncle Dick cursed us as well, and said we would be watched, too. Henceforth, the Department of Fish and Game always suspected me of taking more than my limit of both abalone and lobster and of taking them out of season, too. I was always suspect.

“Pops” Boren had moved to Bird Rock in La Jolla, right on the cliff, and about one hundred feet south of some steps that went down to the ocean. I used to dive at Bird Rock, right in front of Pops’ house. While diving for abalone one day, I saw Frank Felton (another Department of Fish and Game warden) to the south, watching me with his binoculars. Although I knew abalone were out of season, every time I saw one, I popped it loose from its rock, made a show of lifting it into the air and dropped it into my bag. After a display of many abalone, I swam toward Pops' place, but around a corner and out of sight from Felton's view. Unseen by Felton, I took all the abalone out of the sack and put them back in the ocean, scattered under several reefs.

I returned to the beach below Pops' house and yelled up for him to throw me a line. I put my fins, mask and snorkel into my sack and Pops hauled them up to his yard. Then I walked up the steps and was greeted by Felton, who grabbed me and said, "I've finally got you, you son-of-a-bitch!" In the most innocent manner I could muster, I asked what he was raving about. He pulled me by the arm and said another warden was at Pops' house, which was where he was taking me. I obediently went with Felton. We walked into Pops' living room, where the other warden stood with my sack and disgustedly told Felton that it was empty.

Felton, who had watched me fill the sack with abalone, just stood there in embarrassed surprise. Then his face began to turn red, and he screamed that he was going to get me if it took the rest of his life. He was so mad when he slammed out of the house that, when he pulled out of Pops' driveway, he nearly drove his truck into an oncoming car.

I don't know if Felton sustained his efforts to "get me," but I was always strictly legal after that incident with the wardens.

Chapter 18

Kids and Rock Crabs

During the years I was an Ocean Beach lifeguard, many, many kids passed through. Drugs were not yet widely available, so the kids got high from taking off on a big wave or skin diving, sometimes for a real thrill, a little too deep. My relationship with the kids was good, but it was easy. Lifeguards were their heroes. When they thought I was out of earshot, I knew they called me, "Bwana Bob." If one of them got out of line, all I did was take away his surfboard of threaten to call the parents. This was especially effective with the Portuguese kids for whom the threat of their fathers coming after them was terrifying.

If the kids behaved themselves, they were allowed to store their surfboards at the lifeguard tower, ride in the jeep or go diving with me. It was good for them and good for me, because then I could bring in extra limits of abalone or lobster. Many of these kids eventually became excellent divers themselves, providing their families with abundant quantities of seafood.

At the end of each summer, the Ocean Beach lifeguards threw a huge beach party, with all the kids and their families joining in the farewell to another great season. Most of the dinner was pot-luck, brought by the parents, plus we provided trays full of clams, lobster, abalone and fish gathered by the guards and the older kids. We always dug a huge pit in the sand for a bonfire.

As part of this party, at low tide, several kids were sent on a hunt for rock crabs, little crabs with pinchers. A large circle and a smaller, inner, circle was drawn in the sand, and we held crab races to highlight the party. Each contestant selected a crab, which was placed under a bucket in the center circle. The starter would yell, "Go!" Someone lifted the bucket, and the crabs would scatter. The first one to pass the line that marked the outer circle was the winner. For the kids, the fun wasn't so much in whose crab won the race, but in all the splashing and chasing and digging it took to catch them in the first place.

Rock crabs also were the focus of another occasion. One morning, Shitty Smitty and I, with the help of Ricky, Tommy and Fats, caught a bag full of rock crabs, keeping them in sea water until later. After work, we put the crabs into a paper bag and meandered over the Webb's for a few drinks and a little fun.

About nine that evening, a busy night at Webb's, Shitty Smitty and I smuggled our bagged crabs in a paper bag onto the dance floor and dropped the bag. According to plan, the bag broke open and rock crabs scampered everywhere. This, of course, generated a great deal of excitement and screaming and running about, especially among the ladies. Spike Webb, who owned the place, made us retrieve every last one of the crabs and then proceeded to throw us out.

That caper cost me a sack of lobsters to be reinstated as an "acceptable" patron at Webb's. Fortunately, Spike could be very forgiving when lobsters were involved.

In June of 1954, I was completing my last year of college at San Diego State, as a speech and theater major. One of the drama professors, who had stolen away my girlfriend, was directing a campus play, with my former romantic interest in the lead. I was working on the stage crew.

I worked at the beach the day the show opened. As it was a lovely day with clear water and a minus tide, I again enlisted the help of Fats, Ricky and Tommy, and together we collected a bucket of rock crabs.

That night, I took the crabs to the theater, the site of my most recent heartbreak, sneaked them into the building in a paper bag and tossed the bag into the ladies' dressing room. Again, according to plan, the bag burst, and the crabs ran all over the place, causing a small riot. The screams were so loud that a stagehand decided to drop the asbestos curtain to contain the noise backstage.

About five minutes later, I officially arrived to do my job on the stage crew. The director and my former girlfriend knew who was responsible for the crab caper, but no one had actually seen me do anything. I, of course, denied any involvement. The incident scared the shit out of the girls, but the chaos and confusion served the son-of-a-bitch professor right for stealing my sweetheart.

The drama department did manage to get me called up

before the dean, but no one could prove that the crab release was my doing. Sometimes I think I was graduated just so they could get rid of me.

Jon Callahan

Chapter 19

Callahan's Date

Lieutenant Jon Callahan was an officer in the U.S. Navy's elite Underwater Demolition Teams. Jon had been a competitive swimmer in college and was an excellent water man. When not on duty in the Pacific, he was stationed in Coronado at the Naval Amphibious Base. He later became a highly decorated Navy hero, receiving the bronze star for heroic action, leading an underwater demolition team against the Viet Cong.

When Jon and some of his fellow UDT officers were in San Diego, they spent many weekends in Ocean Beach. During the day, they would surf and dive with Willie and me, and at night Shitty Smitty would join us for the inevitable party.

One of these famous parties was a luau, easy since we always seemed to have a ready supply of fresh lobster and abalone. It was the summer I was dating Marylou (not her real name), a lovely lady who was warm of heart and body. Marylou wanted to bring a girlfriend to our luau and asked me to get her a date. Marylou said her friend was plain, but a lot of fun. My friend Callahan didn't have a girl then, so I suggested he be the designated date. I told him she wasn't a looker but was a lot of fun. Callahan's response was, "Sure, fine." So we set it up.

On luau day, when the ladies arrived at the beach, we discovered that Marylou's description of her friend was a monstrous understatement; the poor girl was downright ugly.

Callahan, gentleman that he was, didn't run off, but gave me a look that said I would never again have anything to do with his social life. So, as soon as possible after the ladies arrived, I asked Jane (I'll call her Jane) if she would like a drink. We usually had a five-gallon jug of homemade Portuguese red wine on hand — courtesy of Joe Silva, in exchange for fresh abalone. Jane at first declined, then changed her mind. We later learned the reason for her hesitation.

So we proceeded to drink and eat and drink, consuming generous quantities of lobster, abalone and, especially, wine. Eventually, Callahan and Jane headed out of the house, toward the beach, Callahan with a jug of wine and blanket in one hand and Jane in the other.

To our surprise, about an hour later, without Jane or the wine or the blanket, Callahan came running back to the house blew into the living room and plopped down, wide-eyed and out of breath. I was about to ask where Jane was, when she, too, came running into the house, screaming, "He tried to rape me!" Stunned, I gave Callahan my best "You dirty son of a bitch" look and turned my attention to Jane, who was hysterical and yelling and throwing things and causing such a ruckus we were afraid some neighbor would call the police. So Marylou took her friend into the privacy of the bathroom to settle her down and determine what had happened. But the yelling and commotion continued, and Marylou called me to come and help.

The bathroom was long and narrow, with all the fixtures lined up on one side, the toilet, then the sink, and the tub at the end. When I got there, Jane and Marylou were against the wall. I stood across from them with my back to the commode.

As I tried to calm Jane, she hit me with a left hook, knocking me onto the toilet. I got up, she hit me again, this time with a right, again knocking me onto the toilet.

Well, that was enough. My diplomatic inclinations took a powder. I lost control and hit Jane twice in the jaw, once with a right and once with a left. But she didn't seem to notice, and that scared me.

She just kept yelling and kicking and hitting. Desperate, I yelled for Callahan to come and help. Together, we managed to get the wildly flailing Jane out of the bathroom and into the living room, where we wrestled her to the floor. As she struggled and kicked and screamed, we managed to tie her hands behind her back and her feet together, and then we gagged her.

With Marylou's help, the three of us carried the struggling bundle that was Jane to Marylou's new convertible, where we deposited her onto the back seat. With the top down and Callahan sitting on her, we took Jane back to the La Jolla Beach and Tennis Club where she and Marylou were staying. Their room was upstairs. So, with the car still running to facilitate a quick escape, Callahan and I carried Jane, still tied and gagged, upstairs to the deck in front of their room. I untied her feet, Callahan her arms, and then we ran like hell down the stairs and into the car.

As we were making our hasty retreat, Jane yanked off her gag. We readied ourselves for a repeat of her verbal onslaught at the house. But the effects of the wine apparently had worn off. We were astonished as she yelled down from the deck something about the wonderful time she had had and when would she see us again.

She never did. of course. Callahan certainly never called her. And after that summer, to my dismay, even her friend Marylou was forever absent from Ocean Beach.

Chapter 20

The Birthday Party

It must have been fate that the birthdays of Howard (we called him Al) Pentoney and Willie Meyers were on the same day. In this particular year, on a Saturday. Al was a lawyer with an office above the Strand Theater on Newport Avenue, the main drag in Ocean Beach. He was big, handsome, and an avid fisherman. Willie was my friend and fellow diver who, having learned his trade in the Navy, worked as a commercial hard-hat diver. When not diving, he worked nights as a bartender at Webb's, a local watering hole.

And then there was Shitty Smitty. I don't remember when he first appeared at Ocean Beach, all five feet, five inches of him, overweight and looking like a little Buddha. He was a hard hat diver Willie knew from the Navy. He had big ears and an infectious laugh, which he often followed saying, "bob-bob."

After a long cruise in the western Pacific, Shitty Smitty would just show up with several thousand dollars in his pocket. He loved Webb's, where he was known to set up his beach blanket on the dance floor and have a party, in the middle of the day. Webb's bartender Preacher, who was owner Spike Webb's brother, and everyone else loved Shitty Smitty because he was so funny and because he spent money like the drunken sailor he was. When he had gone through all the funds from his previous cruise, Smitty would borrow just enough to get by from his old shipmate, Willie, and head back out to sea.

It was somehow decided that there would be a surprise birthday party for Al and Willie, and that everybody who was anybody in Ocean Beach would be invited. The site for the party came about because another friend, Hal LaFleur, a real estate developer, had an old house on Santa Monica Street, about a block from the lifeguard station. Hal had plans to tear down the house and build an office complex. Meanwhile, it was just standing vacant.

In preparation for the event, Mousie and I cleaned the inside of the house and moved the old cast iron tub from the bathroom to the center of the living room, to be the ice bucket for the party. An old table was set up for the cake. In keeping with the financial status and organizational skills of everyone involved, the party was strictly a bring-your-own-everything affair, but we provided ice.

I arranged with the local bakery for a large, round birthday cake. When I first called to place the order, specifying to the proud baker that I wanted the cake to be the most bilious-looking thing he could create, he was offended and started yelling obscenities at me over the telephone, initially refusing to fulfill my request for an ugly cake. After about ten minutes of discussion, though, I convinced him it was a joke, and he relented. I even provided him with an old pizza tray for the birthday creation. The completed cake was a work of art. It was a huge, round thing more than two feet across, with orange icing and big, gaudy red roses. It was perfect. It was the ugliest cake I have ever seen.

Everyone we invited was told to dress formally and to bring the birthday boys each a bottle of champagne. All the while, Al and Willie thought it was just another Saturday night affair, although it required far more attention to clothing than usual, and they didn't realize they were the honored guests.

The party was exceptionally well attended. The tiny beach house was filled to overflowing, with nearly one hundred guests, all uncharacteristically decked out in their finest attire.

The ladies came in formal, low-cut gowns, the men in coats and ties. It was an amazing sight for our very laid-back community. We filled the bathtub with ice and everyone's bottles of champagne, played loud Hawaiian music, and drank and danced and drank some more.

About midnight, I asked Tomsie, a former entertainer, to gather the guests around the table and make a speech when I brought out the cake. I would light the two candles, and we would all sing "Happy Birthday" to Al and Willie.

Unknown to the others, when I went into the kitchen for the cake, I modified it, with the able assistance of Shitty Smitty. We tied two cherry bombs together, lifted the cake to remove a big handful from the bottom and inserted the cherry bombs, with a delayed fuse. I had created this delay feature by removing the powder from the fuse, causing it to burn more slowly. After the cherry bombs were inserted into the cake, I lit the slow-burning fuse. It was impossible to tell how long it would be before the fuse burned to the cherry bomb and the orange and red creation exploded.

As I brought out the cake, Tomsie made her speech, then started a rousing chorus of "Happy Birthday." To my dismay, the cake remained intact, with both Al and Willie leaning over it, clutching big butcher knives in anticipation of the cutting ceremony. I pulled the birthday boys away and implored in a whisper, out of earshot of the others, "for Christ's sake, Tomsie, make another speech, this cake's going to blow up and these guys are going to get hurt!" Tomsie enthusiastically began another bombastic round of, "My friends, tonight we are gathered here to celebrate . . ." when the cherry bombs finally exploded, sending cake and icing flying everywhere and all over everyone.

Afterward, not a crumb of cake remained. Tomsie, a lovely lady whose tight, shimmery white, low-cut dress was barely able to contain her ample bosom, was covered everywhere. One of the older and more gallant guests volunteered to lick the cake and icing from her stunning endowments. Tomsie resisted the offer of "help," instead knocking the man flat with a single blow.

Sizing up the situation, Shitty Smitty and I made a hasty retreat out the back door to the beach, not waiting to see the end of the festivities. I later heard the party went on until dawn and was the best ever.

Unfortunately, Tomsie never spoke "to" me again, but I later heard she often spoke "of" me.

Chapter 21

The Rock Off the Rosarito Beach Hotel

About one-half mile offshore from Rosarito Beach, which is about twenty miles south of the U.S. border with Mexico, there is a huge rock that protrudes from the surface of the ocean. In the fifties, it was relatively unknown to Americans as a diving area. So Neil Moyer and I planned a diving trip to see what was there. Neil was a lifeguard friend who introduced me to "real" skin diving and was one of the best I ever dived with. He not only taught me the finer points of diving for abalone, but of eating it, too, as it was his grandmother who prepared the first abalone I ever ate. After that I was hooked!

In August 1953, Neil and I drove down to the Rosarito Beach Hotel, unloaded our diving gear and kicked out from the beach to the rock. In those days we used an inflated inner tube with a gunny sack laced to the tube. As we gathered our lobsters or abalone, we would deposit them into the bag until our return to shore.

On this day, we kicked out to the rock and were delighted to find it loaded with lobster. So we filled our two gunny sacks to overflowing and returned to the beach. Because so many of our lobsters were big, weighing eight to twelve pounds, we took them to a local restaurant to have them cooked. We traded the owner all our lobster in return for preparing as much as we could eat and providing us with beans, tortillas and, most important, beer. We then proceeded to gorge ourselves on as much of our catch as we could wash down with the local cerveza. The owner, or course, was very happy with the deal.

Several years later I again took the skiff from San Diego Bay to dive on the bountiful rock off the Rosarito Beach Hotel, this time with a couple of UDT friends, Doug Allred and George Raines. We all had scuba gear, which by this time was readily available, so instead of starting at the beach, we anchored just off the rock and prepared to dive. I was putting on my single-stage regulator when Doug, who had the same model, asked me how I liked it. I said it was fine. Doug replied that he liked his, too, but he didn't like that it kept blowing bubbles in front of his mask and obscuring his vision. I looked closely at his setup and pretended to study it for awhile. Then, as I fiddled with his regulator, I said I might be able to fix the problem. Slowly and very deliberately, I carefully removed his regulator and rotated it 180 degrees. He had been diving with it upside down! It was an embarrassing moment for a UDT officer.

Doug later became a very successful businessman, and we have remained friends over the years. But I never let him forget the incident with the upside-down regulator.

On our return from the Rosarito Rock, after Doug had learned to use his regulator correctly, we entered San Diego Harbor and headed for Shelter Island. A Navy destroyer passed us, heading toward the open ocean. George was peacefully perched on the starbord stearn rail of the skiff, contentedly watching the world and the Navy destroyer go by when we hit the huge wake of the Navy ship. The skiff tilted sideways and lunged in the water and George, dressed in his Navy foul weather jacket, was tossed overboard like a large rag doll. I wasn't worried about him being in the water, even with all his clothes on. Nevertheless, he was happy to see us turn around and come back for him, although Doug and I were laughing so hard it was difficult to get him into the skiff.

We have never let George forget this.

Willie Myers

Chapter 22

The Cortes Bank

It was the end of lobster season in March 1955 when Whitey, Willie and I set out on Whitey's fishing boat to dive for lobster on the Cortes Bank. The Cortes Bank is about one-hundred miles west of Point Loma, marked by a buoy over Bishop's Rock, which rises from the center of the bank. Bishop's Rock comes within 20 feet of the surface, and when the ocean swell reaches the rock, it picks up and shoulders both right and left. The swell comes from deep water and crests and breaks much like the break at "Overhead" in Ventura, but is even larger and breaks with more force.

Whitey, our captain, was short, dark, handsome and, in his previous life, a successful stock broker. But he had gone through a bitter and costly divorce, said, "Fuck it," bought a thirty-six-foot albacore boat and went fishing.

The other member of our crew for this trip was my buddy, Willie Meyers, a former Navy hard hat diver. By then, he worked days as a commercial diver and sometimes tended bar at night at Webb's, one of our favorite Ocean Beach hangouts.

For this trip, we left Point Loma about eight in the evening and headed west toward the Cortes Bank, under windless conditions and smooth seas. We arrived at our destination about twelve hours later. Conditions were still perfect — clear water, no wind and no swell. Impatient to get wet, Willie and I immediately donned our scuba gear. We needed the tanks because we were after lobsters that were plentiful on the ocean floor, as deep as one-hundred-fifty feet beneath the surface. We plunged into the warm water. Willie went one way, and I went the other, neither of us even considering "buddy diving." After all, we were young, and we were immortal.

God must have been watching over us that day, because if the wind had come up, Whitey, at his post up top managing the boat, would have lost one or both of us. He would have been unable to see our bubbles, and we had no way to signal him. We didn't even have a contingency plan to swim to the Bishop's Rock marker buoy. But we were lucky, so I can proceed with this story.

Willie and I jumped into the water and descended rapidly to the reefs below. As soon as we were on the bottom, we began grabbing lobsters.

To this day, I have never seen so many lobsters at one time. There seemed to be twenty or thirty in every hole and crevice, many weighing ten to twenty pounds. And there were several enormous Jewfish (black sea bass) that followed me around like a small pack of large, hungry dogs. As I reached into a hole, grabbing the two largest lobsters, the others would scatter. Then the Jewfish would swoop in, grab some escapees in their enormous mouths and swim away, with lobster antennas protruding from both sides.

The reef also was covered with pink and white abalone. I hauled a couple dozen back to the boat and, to keep them fresh, threw them into the live bait tank with the lobsters. Willie also was coming up with a great catch of lobster and abalone.

We each made two dives that day, to the limit of our air supply. Under water, we put the lobsters and abalone into gunny sacks tied to inner tubes. We rigged the inner tubes as flotation bags, inflating them from our air tanks. The weight of the lobsters and abalone in the sacks held the open end of the inner tube under water, trapping air in the upper part. In this way, the full gunny sacks would rise to the surface, where Whitey could net them and haul them onto the boat.

We spent the night anchored off the reef, happily anticipating the next day's catch and mentally calculating the capacity of the bait tank. But the wind came up before daylight, making it impossible to dive. So, disappointed, we headed home. But we had a nearly full boat of lobster and abalone, and memories of what we knew was one of the greatest one-day dives of all time.

Returning to San Diego Harbor after dark, we unloaded the bait tank. But only lobsters. There were no abalone anywhere. Only shells! After a few minutes of pulling empty shells out of the tank, we realized that all of the abalone had been eaten by the lobsters. Their shells were all that remained.

Word of the abundant sea life on the Cortes Bank spread rapidly and within a few years was widely known. Enthusiastic commercial dive boat operators, with no limits to worry about, harvested the reef so thoroughly and so frequently that it was soon barren. In later years, our dives yielded only a few small individuals of lobster or abalone.

That is why, today, I am met with mutterings and sidelong glances when I tell the story of our early one-day dive. But I swear it's all true. Just ask Whitey or Willie.

The Author, Coronado Islands, 1954

Chapter 23

Coronado Islands

About seven miles offshore, and ten miles south of the United States-Mexico Boundary Monument, four rocky islets comprise the Coronado Islands. To the west of the most southerly of the four islands, the ocean floor slopes into rocky holes and crevices. It was to this area that Neil Moyer and I made several diving trips for lobster in the early fifties. Neil was a fellow lifeguard and one of the best skin divers I ever knew. He was a good diving partner, as we usually dived without wetsuits or scuba gear. We simply jumped into the water from a boat, equipped with face mask, snorkel and fins, and an inner tube with a gunny sack in the center, where we would store our prey. The most difficult task for these dives was to find someone who would take us to the diving area in a boat that was fast enough to outrun the Mexicans if they came after us.

Diane Justice-Marinos and Bax

In those days, the lobsters were both enormous and plentiful. It was not unusual for one day's efforts to yield ten lobsters, each weighing more than fifteen pounds. The islands also were abundant with large fish. It was not uncommon for the entire ocean surface to be covered with schools of yellowtail or other large game fish. This fishing haven was almost virgin territory, as the sport fishers and other private boats had not yet become frequent visitors.

In addition to diving for lobster at the Coronado Islands, Jon Lindberg, Willie and I made a number of deep dives to salvage anchors that had been dropped by sport boats off the most northeasterly extension of the Coronado Islands, an area known as "Pucky Point." For these excursions, we used scuba gear. A favorite destination of the sport fishers, it was deep and rocky, dropping off to two hundred feet.

To retrieve the lost anchors, we carried a number of rubber inner tubes to lift them off the bottom. We cut a large hole in the bottom of the tube near the valve and two small holes nearby. Through the two small holes, we would string a piece of line, which we attached to the anchor (or other treasure) to be lifted. When the souvenir-of-the-moment was attached, we used one of our mouthpieces to inflate the inner tube with air from the scuba tank. Once the rubber tube started to rise, the air inside expanded, as distance to the surface decreased, carrying the anchor or other object with it, to be picked up by the boat operator. Sometimes it would take three or four inner tubes to lift an anchor off the ocean floor and raise it to the surface.

Looking back on those dives, I now realize we didn't follow any of the standard safety procedures for deep diving. On our last anchor salvage expedition, Jon got the bends and was fortunate to survive. After that, we figured God had been kind enough, and we abandoned our deep diving adventures.

Buzzy Bent, Dave Orrich, John Callahan, Jack Couture, Ron Smith (kneeling)

Chapter 24

Surfing the Tijuana Sloughs With Killer Whales

On the United States side of the international border with Mexico is an area known as the Tijuana Slues. It is a winter surf spot with a north swell that sometimes has a huge break. The slues have formed where the Tijuana River flows into the ocean, creating such a buildup of river sand that the flow of sea water is diverted. This can create ideal surfing conditions.

In winter during the fifties, during a big north swell, the Tijuana Slues was “the place” to surf. On a big day, there could be four breaks at the “Slues,” each one larger with distance from the beach. The first was a powerful shore break. Then there was the second break, the “middle” break and, finally, the outside break, about one-half mile offshore, known to crest at more than twenty feet. The only way to get to the outside break was to paddle out through the rip, then north to the takeoff point.

Denny Holder, a lifeguard at Imperial Beach, always knew the conditions at the Slues. On this particular day in the winter of 1955, word had reached Ocean Beach, via the coconut telegraph, that surf at the Slues was huge. So I called Mouse and Ron Smith, an officer in the Navy Underwater Demolition Teams and part-time lifeguard at Coronado (who, after his Navy service, became a founder of the Chart House restaurants), and we headed south to surf the big swell.

We were not disappointed. By the time we arrived the waves were thirty feet plus. In those days, of course, we had no wetsuits, and leashes for the boards were still in the future. Being winter, the water was about fifty-five degrees. If you fell, you had a long, cold swim to shore to find your board. And you were usually so cold, anyway, that your day was finished. Some surfers would strap fins to their waists in case they needed them to chase their boards to the beach.

On this day, the three of us paddled out through the rip to the outside break to surf the biggest waves. We had been out for about an hour and were sitting outside in the lineup waiting for the next set to come in when we saw a school of killer whales on the surface of the water, coming toward us from the south.

Not much was known about these huge sea creatures then, and we believed they would attack anything in the water — humans, seals, whatever. I was the first to see them coming and called out to Mouse and John. About the same time the whales came into view, a huge set loomed on the horizon. We watched the whales, then the set, then the whales again. Both seemed to be approaching at about the same speed. Fortunately, the waves arrived first. In no mood to be picky, we took off on the first wave to reach us. Not one of us stood, fearful of being separated from his board. We just laid flat and paddled like hell, racing away from the whales and toward the safety of the beach.

We all got in without incident and after awhile longingly considered going back out, as we gazed at set after set of big, well-formed waves that just kept rolling into shore. But the whale-sighting had scared the hell out of us, enough to end our surfing that day at the Slues.

We later learned that killer whales generally do not attack humans.

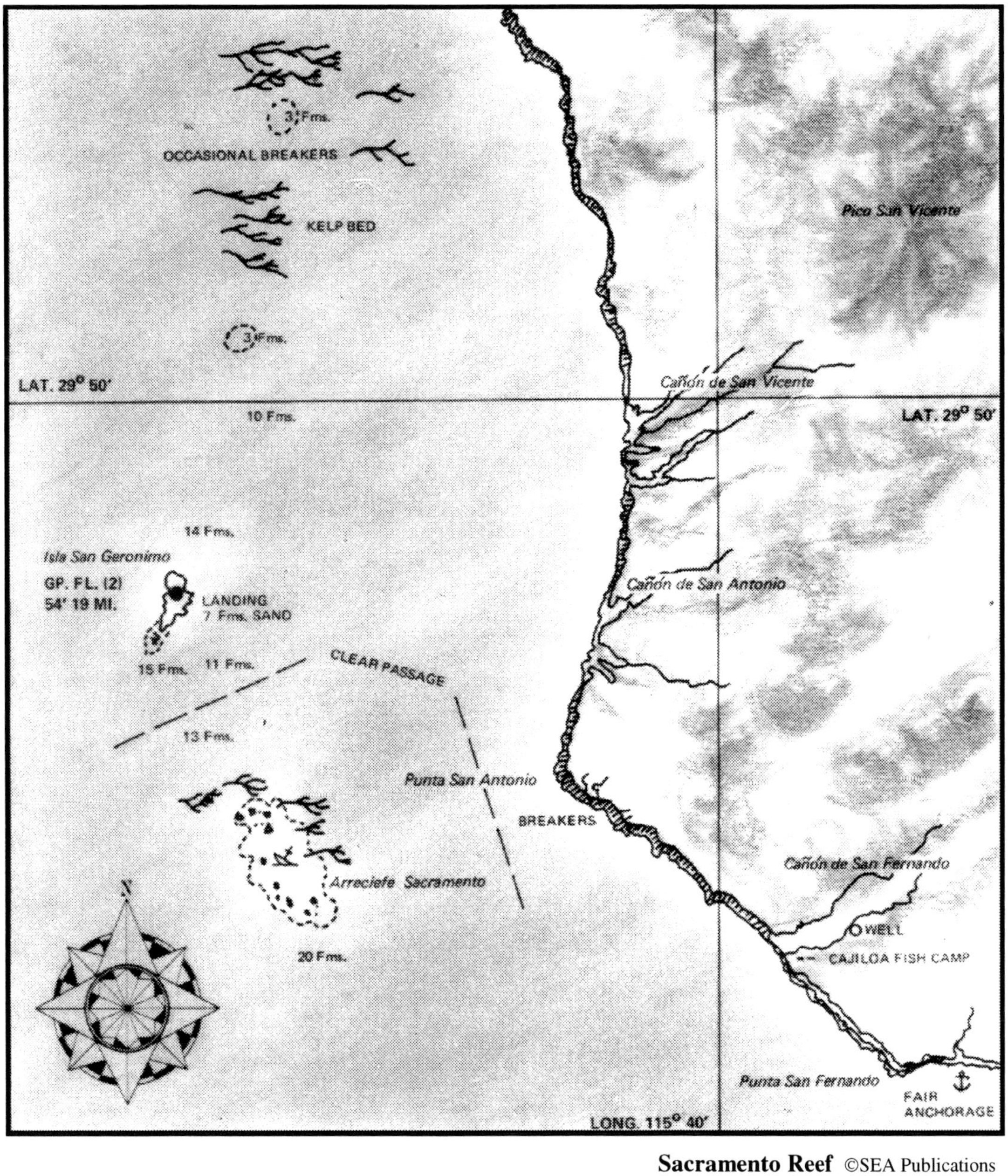

Sacramento Reef ©SEA Publications

Chapter 25

The Sacramento Reef

On the ocean side of the Baja Peninsula, about nine miles south of Punta Baja (about two hundred miles south of Point Loma), lies a small island called "Geronimo." About one-and-one-half miles to the southeast and five miles offshore of Geronimo lies the Sacramento Reef, directly in the path of any north-bound vessels tracking close to the coast. Historians say there are more ships lying wrecked on this reef than anywhere else on the entire Pacific Coast. The reef covers an area of about two-and-one-half square miles, with a narrow area about two hundred yards long that, at low tide, is fully exposed. The reef is named after the two-hundred-seventy-one-foot side-wheeler, the S.S. Sacramento, which in 1872 struck it and sank while carrying passengers from Panama to the California gold rush.

Tad Devine, son of character actor Andy Devine and graduate of Stanford University, was an officer in the Navy Underwater Demolition Teams. I had met Tad before his Navy service when he was a lifeguard in Los Angeles. While in the Navy, he was stationed primarily at the Navy Amphibious Base at Coronado. Tad and fellow officers George Raines and John Callahan formed the core group that spent many of their weekends with me, surfing and diving at Ocean Beach and Sunset Cliffs.

Tad said he had learned from a reliable source that, when the S.S. Sacramento wrecked on the reef, it had been loaded with gold. So in August 1958, ignoring the backward logic of the story, we organized a diving trip to the reef. We were going to find the gold and be rich.

The crew for this expedition was Devine, Raines, Callahan, Bob Terry (their executive officer, who would not let them go unless he was

Walt Slaunger, George Raines, Jon Callahan, Bob Terry, Willie Meyer, the Author

invited), Willie Meyers, Walt Slaunger (who owned the fishing boat, "Milida"), Lamar "Pops" Boren and me.

We left San Diego Harbor early in the morning and traveled down the coast past Ensenada, stopping for the night in the lee of San Martin Island, a few miles north of the entrance to San Quintin. Early the next morning when I came on deck, Walt was already fishing for bass. I selected from his collection of poles, and soon both of us were pulling in fish from the back of the boat. In less than an hour, we caught enough to provide breakfast for everyone. We feasted on fresh fish and bad coffee, then continued on to our destination.

We arrived while it was still daylight and anchored for the night on the reef. We would move the Milida away and into deeper water in the morning. With hunger and dinner-time fast approaching, I popped into the water with scuba gear and got about ten abalone, enough for the evening's feast. The next day, and the next, and the next, the weather was perfect, and we spent all three days diving the reef for buried treasure.

Jon Callahan, Willie Meyers, Andy Devine, George Raines

Over the years, the story of who got which lobster changes, based on who is doing the telling. In truth, I was the only one throwing lobsters into the boat, as everyone else wanted to save space for the buried treasure they expected to find. It turned out that the only "treasure" we found were pieces of brass from the various wrecks on the reef, which Pops picked up.

Tad found a large object that looked like a boiler plate from the old S.S. Sacramento. He ascended to the surface faster than was really safe, and when he broke water yelled, "Gold!" Pops and I followed him back down and congregated on the ocean floor in anticipation of riches. As we inspected Tad's find, we discovered it wasn't gold, but a series of brass plates that had, over the years been polished by the ocean currents and the sand shifting back and forth across them over the year. It was so heavy we couldn't haul it to the surface, but we found another treasure—a large boiler in shallow water. Together, we were able to swim the boiler to the surface and load it and ourselves into the IBS. Then we took our treasure out to the Milida, anchored safely away from the reef in about fifty feet of water.

Unfortunately, in the process of transferring the boiler out of the IBS into the Milida, we drowned it. Pops had a fit, jumping up and down on the deck of the Milida and yelling for us to go get it. So we decided to go bring it back up. Because the water was deep, Raines donned a scuba tank and went to the bottom with a rope.

The plan was to tie the rope to the boiler and then haul it up to the Milida, as it was too heavy to be carried to the surface.

Everything went smoothly. George descended to the bottom, Devine and I stayed in the water on the surface with masks and snorkels, and Callahan and Pops waited on the Milida. We planned to grab the line, swim the boiler to the side of the Milida, and then let Pops and Callahan haul it up into the boat.

Everything went as smooth as silk until Raines was almost to the surface, but he stopped about ten feet below us. The rope was too short, and the boiler was too heavy for Raines to pull it off the bottom alone. And he was now crossing his hand across his throat, the universal diver's signal that he was running out of air.

Lamar with the boiler in the background

Devine and I pretended we didn't understand, but Raines was looking desperate. So, we dove to his rescue, took the rope, and together the three of us lifted the boiler far enough off the bottom to get the rope to the surface, where we could all breathe. The rest of the crew came to our assistance in the IBS and hauled the boiler the rest of the way to the surface and, once more, into the inflatable. Our second attempt to transfer it to the Milida was successful.

After the trip, Pops kept the boiler. When he died, I told his kids how it had been acquired, and they gave it to me. So, in the end, we didn't find any gold, but I still have the boiler that almost drowned George Raines.

Chapter 26

Webb's and Big Al and Law School

Webb's was a popular bar and nightclub on the southeast corner of Newport Avenue and Bacon Street. Owned by Spike Webb, his brother, Preacher, and nephew, Mike Drensky, worked as bartenders. Webb's was also the hangout of Howard (Al) Pentoney, the lawyer whose office was upstairs over the Strand theater. Al was a big, handsome man in his mid thirties, a fine trial lawyer, a great fisherman and an even greater carouser.

One Saturday in early June, I happened into Webb's after work, at about five in the evening. Big Al was already there, with another well-known lawyer (I'll call him Joe, because he is now a federal judge and would likely deny this story). They had just come from the annual San Diego County Bar Association picnic. In those days, it was requisite for participants at such occasions to engage in much serious drinking, so the two were feeling no pain. And both still were dressed for the picnic — shirts, short pants and flip-flops. Spike introduced us, and the fun continued for another hour. Then he kicked Al and Joe out of the place because of Webb's policy: patrons couldn't be in the bar in short pants after six in the evening.

It was nothing personal. Nevertheless, Al was livid and put up quite a scene. Joe wasn't ready to leave either, regardless of the dress code. So I intervened to solve the problem. We walked down the street to my house next to the lifeguard station. I provided Big Al with a pair of jeans that extended to just above his ankles. Joe still presented a problem, because I had only two pair of long pants and they were now both in use. The problem was solved when I produced a long Japanese kimono that a grateful lady friend had given me. Now, thus dressed, we returned to Webb's.

Spike thought he had gotten rid of us and was sore that the drunks had returned but, as Al pointed out, we now complied with the after-six requirements. Joe and Al proceeded to get drunker and rowdier as the evening wore on. Joe became enamored with a song on the juke box, put in five dollars, and played it about 100 times. Meanwhile, Al seemed to get louder and more abusive with each drink. Finally, about nine in the evening, we were thrown out again, this time on the merits of our drunken behavior, not our attire.

Both Al and Joe had had a long day. Although they could still walk, they had trouble standing. Being somewhat less intoxicated than my two new friends, I volunteered to drive them home. I would borrow the lifeguard cliff rig. After all, both men lived nearby, on the bay side of North Mission Beach, Joe near Carmel Point and Al a few blocks to the north. So we meandered to the lifeguard station where we sort of fell into the big pickup truck, with boom attached to the back and painted international orange. We roared away from the beach with red light flashing and siren blasting.

As we approached Joe's through the alley, lights and siren announcing our arrival, a large group of people came pouring out of his house to see what disaster had occurred. When we got to the house I stopped, and we pushed Joe out, still wearing my kimono. Then we sped off down the alley toward Al's. Fortunately, Al's wife and neighbors were used to such diversions, so there was no fuss at his place.

Then I drove back to Ocean Beach, without the light and siren, put away the truck and retired, thanking my lucky stars that this trip had not been noticed by any "officials."

I later learned that Joe was supposed to have been home by six because he and his wife were entertaining friends for dinner. But when he got out of the cliff rig, he just walked by all of his guests, who had been waiting for three hours, stumbled upstairs and went to sleep in a bathtub. Although he later became a close friend, to this day Joe still hasn't returned my kimono.

Another time, I was again in Webb's, this time with Al, who was enjoying himself and needling Mike, who was tending bar. Mike just played along, insisting that nothing Al or I could say to him could ever make him mad. Al considered that a challenge, and he went to work on Mike. Well, nobody was a match for Al, especially when his lawyer's demeanor and skills were lubricated by abundant quantities of alcohol. After only thirty minutes of abuse from Al, Mike reached his patience threshold, jumped over the bar and started throwing punches. So Preacher called the police.

Soon, two young, uniformed officers arrived, ushered Al and

me outside and pinned us against the wall by the front door. All the while, Al struggled and hollered and insisted they read us our rights. He caused enough of a fuss that the young officers finally called for backup.

Our guardian angel must have been watching over us that night. Because when the third officer arrived, it was Sergeant Kelly. Just that afternoon, I had given Kelly a bag of lobsters, fresh from my daily dive. What was he to do following such generosity from me?

He took one look at us, shook his head, and called the rookie cops aside for a conference. After a few minutes, the rookies left. Kelly came back and issued his directive: "I want you two assholes to get out of here, and if I see you again tonight I'm not going to arrest you, I'm going to shoot you!" The speed with which we left the scene was impressive.

Afterward, it occurred to me that if big Al had not demanded that we be advised of our constitutional rights, the patrol officers would probably have not called for the Sergeant. Instead, they would have arrested us. That got me to thinking that maybe I ought to find out more about these constitutional rights.

So I started showing up at Al's office in the evening, after my day as a beach lifeguard, to read his law books.

Eventually I decided that maybe this could be a worthwhile pursuit. And the rest, as they say, is history.

Thanks, Al.

We have seen the encircling sea surge on
with its uncertainties, its graces;
We have dived deep, taken abalone,
gathered black coral, harvested the sea.
We have watched sick gulls die, and live ones soar;
We have looked with new wonder on the world.
(Charles Faust)

Author 1956

Chapter 27

Conclusion

This book covers some of the more interesting events that occurred during my tenure as a lifeguard at Ocean Beach. I have omitted the romantic incidents that happened over these years out of respect to all those marvelous ladies and from fear of being accused of gross exaggerations. Besides, Captain Hardy would think it in bad taste to name names.

None of my friends, and no acquaintances from the beach, gave me any chance of finishing law school, much less of passing the California Bar. And, except for Mouse who once asked me to help with an adoption, very few of them ever requested assistance with their legal problems as they feared the worst, based on my previous behavior. They refused to believe that I could really have become a lawyer, much less a competent one. I did notice things changed somewhat after I became a Superior Court judge. By then, I think, they started giving me the benefit of the doubt.

Now that I have retired from the bench and celebrated my 69th birthday, I look back fondly on those carefree years at the beach. And I understand Sterling Hayden, in his introduction to *The Wanderer*, when he said no matter what happened in his life, he would not change places with anyone, and then quoted H. Sewall Bailey:

"... But I think he swaggered
so that he could pretend
the other side of nowhere
led to somewhere in the end."

- H. Sewall Bailey

Ocean Beach-San Diego, California: 1998

Where Are They Now?

Calvin (Spade) Burns died in 1991 at the age of 93. In 1936 Spade was forced to retire because of a serious injury he received while making a rescue. After leaving the lifeguards he became a commercial fisherman and made a dramatic rescue in his late 80's when the boat he was on sank at sea.

John Brennen is 78 and lives in Ocean Beach. He worked for both the City and County lifeguards and later in the office of the San Diego City Managers Office.

Richard (Storm Surf) Taylor worked for the City Lifeguards in the forties. He has passed on to a better world and is surfing big waves, we believe, in heaven.

Raymond (Skeeter) Malcolm was 71 when he died in 1993 after retiring as a San Diego City School principal. Skeeter set an example for all surfers for kindness and courtesy.

Lamar Boren died in 1986 after a brilliant career as a cinematographer in movies and television including, "Sea Hunt", "Underwater", "Old Man and the Sea", "The Day of the Dolphin" and several James Bond movies.

Maynard Hetherly was 37 when he died in 1962. He was one of the most interesting characters that ever hit the beach. Where ever he is I know he is having fun.

Charles W. Hardy was 59 when he died in 1968. He had been Lifeguard Captain for 38 years. He became "Chief Police/Lifeguard" in 1936 when Spade Burns was forced to quit because of a severe injury he received while making a rescue.

Jack Prodonovich is 85. He retired from the San Diego City Schools System in 1972, and still dives and makes spear guns. He lives in Point Loma with his wife Gertrude of 57 years.

Wally Potts is 80. He worked for Solar as an engineer until he retired in 1978. He lives in Ocean Beach with his wife Vi of 60 years.

Leonard Cooper must be in his early sixties and is seen every once in a while riding his Hog in Ocean Beach.

Dick Ryan died in 1972 . His widow Peggy lives in San Marcos. Ricky is 51. He became a minister and lives in Santa Barbara. Knowing Ricky gives one faith that maybe there is a God. Tommy is 49. He is a landscaper and lives in El Cajon.

James (Mouse) Robb is 65. He was a lifeguard for two years in the fifties, then went to work for Western Electric until he retired in 1986. He and his wife Carol live in Ocean Beach. Mouse still surfs almost every day, dives when the water is clear and gabs with me over coffee every morning at 5:00 a.m. at the "Sea Trader" on Point Loma Avenue in Ocean Beach.

Doug Smith is 63 and lives in Ocean Beach. He remained a lifeguard and retired on disability. He was, and still is, one of the handsomest men I ever knew.

Gus Petro was 57years old when he died. He left the lifeguards and had a distinguished career in sales.

Don Mellon is 65 and lives in Point Loma. After leaving the lifeguards he became a successful real estate developer.

Brad (Fats) Sandborn is 51 and lives in Hawaii. He became a meat man at a super market and now runs a hamburger stand on the beach in Maui. I suggested he name it after Mrs. Miller but ASack=s@ won.

Gena Grigg sold her house at Muscle Beach and moved to Maui where she painted until her death several years ago.

Richard W. Grigg (Ricky) is 61 years old. He worked as a lifeguard in Santa Monica in the fifties. He graduated from Stanford in 1958, received his Masters from the University of Hawaii in 1963 and his PHD from Scripps Institution of Oceanography in 1970. He has published hundreds of scientific articles, written several books and is considered on of the worlds great surfers. He is a full professor at the University of Hawaii and lives in Honolulu with his wife.

Robin Grigg-Smith is 66 years old. She was on of the first great women board surfers and a champion in the outrigger canoes. She graduated from Stanford and is a physical therapist living in Honokaa, Hawaii.

John Callahan is 65. He has been married to Michelle for 38 years. After leaving the Navy in 1968 (he was a highly decorated Seal officer) he went to work for the Chart House Restaurants. He currently is the manager of the Chart House in Newport, Rhode Island.

<u>Willie Meyers</u> is 70 years old and lives in Fort Lauderdale, Florida. He still works as a commercial diver, boat operator and a marine consultant.

<u>Brendan (Hevs) McCellan</u> who entertained beach goers for years, died several years ago, and is now entertaining those of his friends who also made it to Heaven.

<u>Jon Lindbergh</u> is 67 and lives near Seattle, Washington. He still dives, and raises cranberries in Chile.

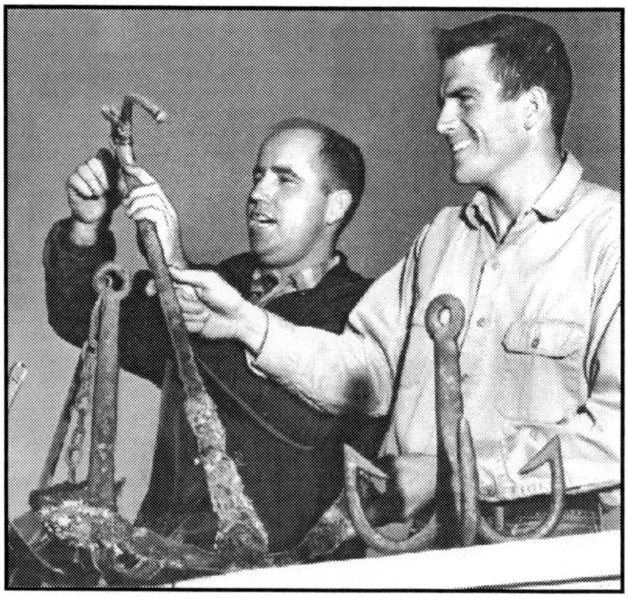

Tad Devine is 64. He left the Navy UDT in 1960. He stayed in the Navel reserve for several years rising to the rank of Lieutenant Commander. He lives in Newport Beach, California with his wife Donna of 36 years (which in its self is remarkable). Over the years Tad has bought and sold several businesses and currently sits on the board of directors of School Boards and businesses.

Ron Smith is 65 and lives in Del Mar. He left the Navy UDT in 1963 and became an owner of the Chart House Restaurants. He is also a world class triathlete and still consults for Chart House. He has been married so many times that there isn't enough space for their names.

George Raines is 64 He was an officer in the Navy UDT. After the Navy he became a stock broker and retired after a very successful career. He has been married to Sheilla for 35 years which is his most remarkable achievement.

Doug Allred is 63and lives in Del Mar, California. He has been married to Ann for 47 years. He left the Navy UDT in 1960 and became a well-known developer and an owner of the San Diego Tennis & Racket Club.

Neil K. Moyer is 64. He became Lifeguards Lieutenant and later worked for the San Diego City Mangers office as a lobbyist in Sacramento. After leaving the City he became and still is a very successful real estate investor.

Little Mike , I suspect, grew up to be president of a large computer company and spends a lot of time with his children.

Malcolm the Mooch is still missing some where north of San Diego.

May Britt married Sammy Davis, Jr., and still lives somewhere.

May and Mrs. Miller have passed on to Hamburger Heaven and compete daily.

Acknowledgment

My thanks to Carolyn Trindle-Smith who assisted me by editing this work. Her help was invaluable. To John Brennan, Marion Baker, Bill Martin, Norma Malchom, Jack Podonovich and Diane Justice-Marinos for supplying photographs. To Alfred Pagano of Giant Photos for producing the negatives of the works in this book and to Dan Tororoski for advice and help with my computer. To Kathleen Blavatt for her help in reproducing the photographs and David Marlow at WhitMar Electronic Press for his expert printing of this work. Finally to Charles R. Faust for his original drawings, ideas and encouragement.

Framed quality enlargements (to size specified) of the photographs appearing in this work may be purchased through Tom Sandler at the Frame Station, 1011 Ft. Stockton Drive, San Diego, CA 92103
(619) 298-8558.

A publication of the Sunset Cliffs Literary, Poetry, and Philosophical Society of Ocean Beach, California